SANTA ANA PUBLIC LIBRARY

3 1994 01514 0806

D1092189

The Glassfibre Handbook

The Glassfibre Handbook

R.H.WARRING

666.157 WAR
Warring, R. H.
The Glassfibre handbook

CENTRAL $10.95
               3 1994 0 15140806

SPECIAL INTEREST MODEL BOOKS

Special Interest Model Books Ltd.
P.O. Box 327
Poole
Dorset
BH15 2RG

First published by Argus Books Ltd, 1983
Reprinted 1987, 1989, 1991, 1993, 1996, 1997, 2000
Reprinted by Special Interest Model Books Ltd 2003, 2004, 2006, 2008, 2010, 2012.

www.specialinterestmodelbooks.co.uk

© R. H. Warring 2003

The right of R. H. Warring to be identified as the Author
of this work has been asserted by him in accordance
with the Copyright, Designs and Patents Act of 1988.

All rights reserved. No part of this book may be
reproduced in any form by print, photography, microfilm
or any other means without written permission from the
publisher.

ISBN 978 0 85242 820 7

Printed and bound in Malta by Melita Press

Contents

		page
INTRODUCTION – HOW TO USE THIS HANDBOOK		6
CHAPTER 1. HOW GRP WAS BORN – BY ACCIDENT!		7
CHAPTER 2. FABRICATION TECHNIQUES		9
CHAPTER 3. GLASS FIBRE MATERIALS		13
CHAPTER 4. RESINS		21
CHAPTER 5. ACCELERATORS, CATALYSTS AND CURING		29
CHAPTER 6. OTHER MATERIALS		36
CHAPTER 7. QUANTITIES REQUIRED		44
CHAPTER 8. TOOLS AND EQUIPMENT		48
CHAPTER 9. DESIGN IN GRP		53
CHAPTER 10. MAKING MOULDS		59
CHAPTER 11. HAND LAY-UP		65
CHAPTER 12. MOULDED SHAPES		73
CHAPTER 13. CASTING, POTTING AND ENCAPSULATION		81
CHAPTER 14. GRP 'AT HOME'		86
CHAPTER 15. TRANSPARENT AND TRANSLUCENT PANELS		90
CHAPTER 16. TANKS IN GRP		93
CHAPTER 17. GARDEN POOLS AND FISHPONDS		98
CHAPTER 18. GRP IN MODEL MAKING		103
CHAPTER 19. GRP HULLS		110
CHAPTER 20. SANDWICH CONSTRUCTION		116
CHAPTER 21. SHEATHING HULLS		121
CHAPTER 22. GRP CAR BODIES		123
CHAPTER 23. CAR BODY REPAIRS		128
CHAPTER 24. REPAIRS TO GRP		132
CHAPTER 25. FAULTS, CAUSES AND REMEDIES		139
APPENDIX 1. HOW THICK?		144
2. HOW STRONG?		148
3. HOW HEAVY?		153
4. RESISTANCE TO CHEMICALS, etc.		154
5. AGEING EFFECTS		155
6. THERMAL PROPERTIES OF GRP LAMINATES		157
7. OSMOSIS		158
8. RESIN TECHNOLOGY		159
9. DEFLECTIONS AND STRESSES IN SANDWICH BEAMS		160

Introduction

The majority of readers will be concerned only with hand lay-up methods of producing glassfibre laminates and mouldings (and repair work using GRP), and in casting methods. The practical descriptions on how-to-do-it are thus confined to these two basic techniques. Other methods used in commercial productions are described only briefly to complete a picture of the full scope of working with glassfibre and other reinforcement materials.

Each chapter is complete in itself, so to use the book as a practical guide simply turn to the subject which is of immediate interest which will normally contain all the information necessary to get working on a particular project. It is recommended, however, that Chapters 3, 4, 5 and 6 are worth reading first to give a good background knowledge about the materials involved, and also Chapter 8 for detailing necessary tools and equipment. Chapter 7 will also be a most useful reference for estimating the quantities of materials required for any job (although for simple repair work you can usually buy the necessary materials in the form of a kit). If you need more information on the detail design of glassfibre projects, then use Chapter 9 as a guide.

The more technical aspects of glassfibre laminate properties, etc., are covered in the Appendix section. This again has been divided into short, individual sections so that you can go straight to the sort of information you require. Equally you can ignore them. You can produce quite satisfactory glassfibre work without getting involved in technicalities at all. But this further information is there should you need it.

Acknowledgements

Numerous individuals, companies and authorities have assisted in the compilation of this definitive work on glassfibre or GRP as it is usually called (see Chapter 1). In particular the author would like to acknowledge the help provided by Fibreglass Limited, Fothergill & Harvey plc, Industrial Textiles Division, and Glassplies of Southport.

CHAPTER ONE

How GRP was born
—by accident!

Some of the earliest Egyptian glass vessels used as containers for oils and perfumes were built up from glass fibres laboriously spun by hand around glazed cores of clay, and very closely packed so as to be 'watertight'. Later, with the introduction of glass blowing, the use of glass fibres was restricted to decorating glassware, many fine examples of which are to be seen in museums. Coloured glass fibres appeared in the last century and were widely used for decorating ornaments. Particular examples—again to be seen in museums—are glass birds with 'silk' tails of coloured glass fibres.

Then a little less than a century ago the first commercial process for mass producing glass 'silk' (glass fibre) was established in Germany. It was not until 1930 that the first commercial glass 'silk' was produced in the U.K. in Scotland, and 1938 before the first commercial production of continuous filament glass by Owens Corning Fiberglass in the U.S.A.

It was this production of continuous glass filament which could be formed into yarns, tapes and cloth that turned glass fibre from a 'decorative' material into an 'engineering' material, used particularly for insulation of electric motor windings. Then in the early 1940s a sample of catalysed polyester resin was accidentally spilt over several layers of glass cloth which hardened overnight into a new material—glass reinforced resin. The reinforced plastics industry was born and during the war glass reinforced plastics (GRP) were used for making radomes, fuel tank backing and body armour mouldings—all based on glass *fabric* reinforcement.

The start and subsequent development of glass reinforced materials depended on two things: the ready availability of glass fibre in a suitable, easily handled form for reinforcement, and a 'hard' *thermoset* synthetic resin which cured at normal room temperatures by the addition of a chemical catalyst.

Today there is a wide range of such *cold*-setting thermoset resins available for use with various glass fibre materials for reinforcement. Glass fibre reinforcement is also used with *heat*-setting thermoset resins (curing under heat and pressure) and also with *thermoplastic* resins. The basic difference between these two types of resins is that the *thermoset* types are only 'plastic' in their formulative stage and once 'cured', set hard by an irreversible process of change. They then have relatively stable mechanical properties, unaffected by heat unless this is sufficiently high to cause them to char or burn. *Thermoplastic* resins, on the other hand, may have even better strength at normal temperatures, but readily soften and lose that strength with increasing temperature until they eventually melt at relatively low temperatures. In other words they are not thermally 'set'—heat can change them into a liquid state, setting to a solid state again on cooling.

Why call it GRP?

All synthetic resins are man-made materials or *polymers,* coming under the general description *plastics.* All plastics have one thing in common. They lack the strength of metals and other 'strong' materials. Also thermoset resins are relatively brittle, and thermoplastic resins are relatively elastic. About the only way a resin can be made both strong and rigid is by combination with a reinforcing material.

In the case of glass fibre used as a reinforcing material the combination is a Glass Fibre Reinforced Plastic, or GFRP for short. This is usually abbreviated to GRP (glass reinforced plastic).

There are, however, variations on this abbreviated description. In America all glass fibre materials are referred to as Fiberglass—so instead of GRP, the designation *FRP* is normally used (fiberglass reinforced plastic) or just Fiberglass. In the U.K. Fibreglass (with a different spelling of 'fibre') is a registered trade name of Fibreglass Ltd., the foremost manufacturer of glass fibres in Britain (and one of the three largest reinforcement manufacturers in Europe). In their literature, this company invariably refer to GRP as FRP (Fibreglass reinforced plastic).

What about other 'RPs'?

Glass fibre is by no means the only reinforcement material used with plastics. Paper, for example, is widely used in the production of high strength laminates in sheet form—generally referred to as *laminated plastics* rather than RP (reinforced plastic) materials.

Closely allied to GRP, however, two alternative reinforcing materials are finding increasing application—carbon fibre and aramid fibre (Kevlar). Such composite materials are described as CFRP (carbon fibre reinforced plastic); and AFRP (aramid fibre reinforced plastics) or KRP (Kevlar reinforced plastic), respectively. In America, when 'Fiberglass' is commonly quoted instead of GRP (or FRP), Kevlar is the common description for its aramid fibre counterpart.

Given other reinforcing materials, which will inevitably appear, the same letter designation will follow—the initial letter or letters describing the reinforcing material precisely, ending with . . . RP.

CHAPTER TWO

Fabrication techniques

Various different techniques are possible for producing laminates or mouldings in GRP. Of these, hand lay-up is the commonest method used commercially, as well as being the only technique normally used for amateur work. Some of the other techniques are, however, adaptable and may be worth considering for special jobs.

Hand Lay-up (Fig. 2.1)

Also known as *contact moulding*, this is the process using a male or female mould. After mould preparation with a release agent and gel coat, reinforcing material is placed on or in the mould, wetted out with catalysed resin and consolidated.

Hand lay-up is a simple, effective process with no size limitations, and produces a high gloss finish on one surface. Its only real limitations are that there is only one finished surface, and the quality of the product is very much dependent on the operator.

Spray-up (Fig. 2.2)

Spray-up is essentially similar to hand lay-up except that catalysed resin and chopped glass rovings are sprayed simultan-

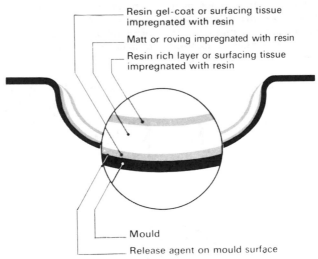

Resin gel-coat or surfacing tissue impregnated with resin

Matt or roving impregnated with resin

Resin rich layer or surfacing tissue impregnated with resin

Mould

Release agent on mould surface

FIG. 2.1 HAND LAY-UP

9

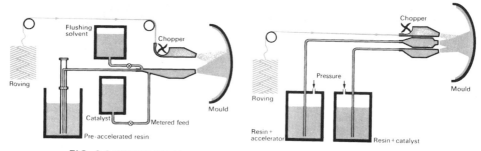

FIG. 2.2 SPRAY-UP METHODS—Single pot (left) and two-pot (right)

eously on to the mould surface by a special gun until the required thickness is built up and then rolled to consolidate. It is used commercially where high production rates are required. Quality of the product is very dependent on the skill of the operator.

Filament Winding (Fig. 2.3)

This is a method of producing low weight mouldings of circular or near-circular cross-section. The mould in this case takes the form of a mandrel which can be rotated to wind on spiralling layers of glass roving, fabric or narrow width mats. Catalysed resin is then applied on the mandrel, or in commercial production by pulling the reinforcement through resin before winding.

Bag Moulding (Fig. 2.4)

With *bag-moulding* a female mould is used into which the laminate is laid up by hand, or by spray-up. The laminate is then covered with a flexible rubber sheet, clamped to the sides of the mould. This rubber sheet is then drawn into intimate contact with the laminate by applying suction (vacuum bag moulding), or air pressure (pressure bag moulding). This replaces consolidation of the laminate by rollering.

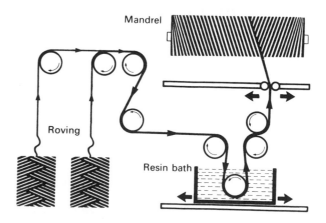

FIG. 2.3 FILAMENT WINDING

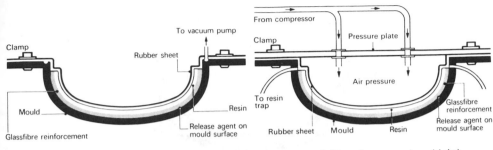

FIG. 2.4 BAG MOULDING TECHNIQUES—Vacuum bag (left) and pressure bag (right)

COLD PRESS MOULDING

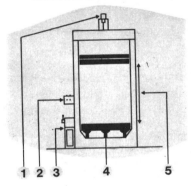

1. Top coarse-drive motor
2. Electric control
3. Pressure applied by hydraulic ram
4. Available daylight
5. Hydraulic control

FIG. 2.5

Cold Press Moulding (Fig. 2.5)

Cold press moulding uses simple presses and lightweight tools. Reinforcement material is placed in the tools and catalysed resin poured in. The tools are then closed and the pressure produced spreads the resin through the moulding, and at the same time consolidates it.

A particular advantage of this method is that it produces GRP mouldings with two finished surfaces.

Hot Press Moulding (Fig. 2.6)

This is similar to cold press moulding, except that the tools are heated. It is capable of high production rates but requires expensive tooling. It is only used for high production runs. Cost otherwise is unjustified.

Resin Injection (Fig. 2.7)

Resin injection involving the use of matched moulds. Only the glass fibre reinforcement is placed in the mould which is then closed and catalysed resin is either blown or sucked into the mould, displacing and replacing all the air (and at the

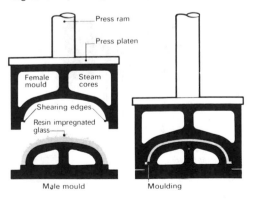

FIG. 2.6 HOT PRESS MOULDING

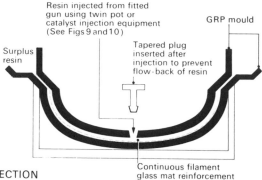

Resin injected from fitted gun using twin pot or catalyst injection equipment (See Figs 9 and 10)

GRP mould

Surplus resin

Tapered plug inserted after injection to prevent flow-back of resin

FIG. 2.7 RESIN INJECTION

Continuous filament glass mat reinforcement

same time wetting out the glass reinforcement).

Injection Moulding fig. 2.8)

This is a normal injection moulding process as used with thermoplastics. Raw materials used are pre-compounded pellets of the plastic together with glass fibre.

INJECTION MOULDING

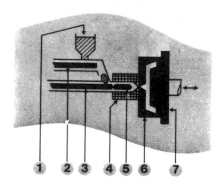

1. *Moulding compound*
2. *Charging ram*
3. *Injection ram*
4. *Heating element*
5. *Spreader*
6. *Female mould*
7. *Male mould*

FIG. 2.8

The product is a glass reinforced thermoplastic moulding—often described as glass-filled—e.g. glass-filled nylon.

Continuous Processes

Commercially certain GRP products are also capable of being produced by a continuous process. Much—if not all—of the ready-made GRP sheeting (plain or corrugated) available at DIY shops is produced by a continuous method involving impregnating a travelling layer of chopped strand, fabric, chopped roving, etc. with catalysed resin, sandwiching it between two sheets of cellulose film and passing it through rollers and finally through a curing oven. The cured sheet emerges as a continuous length.

The other commercial method of continuous production is *pultrusion* where the reinforcement material is in the form of continuous glass roving or twisted yarn fed over rollers through a resin bath and then through a heated forming die. This is an economic method of producing rod or similar 'solid' stock of any required cross section in a continuous length.

Neither method is suitable for amateur work. They are mentioned for the sake of completeness.

CHAPTER THREE

Glass fibre materials

There are many different types of glass, but for practical reinforcement only six types are produced in fibre form. Out of these only one is used on a very wide scale. This is *'E' glass*, or electrical grade, which has excellent all-round properties and is suitable for almost all applications. The other common type *'A' glass* or alkali glass is a little lighter and nearly as strong, but far less water resistant than 'E' glass. Being cheaper it was originally used for GRP mouldings, but is no longer in commercial production. All the other glass types are specials with only a limited production in fibre form. These are *'C' glass*—a special chemical-resistant type—*'S' glass* and *'R' glass*—special high-strength types used where very high performance is required (e.g. in mouldings for aerospace applications). Also *high modulus glasses* based on beryllia which are heavier and less 'elastic' than other glass fibres.

Some comparative properties of these different type glasses are given in Table I.

Glass Fibre Sizes

Glass fibre is produced in a range of filament diameters and strand dimensions to close tolerances for different uses. Typical size ranges for reinforcement materials are:—

Rovings and chopped strands—8-14μm (.0003-.0006in).

Chopped strand mats—9-14μm (.00035-.0006in).

Special rovings — 10-15μm (.0004-.0006in).

Continuous strand mats — 14-15μm (.0006in).

Reinforcement fabrics—4-10μm (.00016-.0004in).

Initial Treatment

All glass fibres must be treated with a liquid size when produced, the choice of sizing being a critical part of the product of glass fibre reinforcement materials. The size must not only protect the glass from abrasion whilst it is being drawn but also acts as a process aid during moulding. A typical 'forming' size used on reinforcement fibres comprises:—

A keying agent to promote adhesion between the matrix and the glass. An organic silicon compound is most frequently used.

A film former, usually a polymer in emulsion form. In the past this has frequently been polyvinyl acetate.

A lubricant, usually acid amides.

Other materials added to give specific properties, such as anti-static, etc.

Reinforcement Materials

Continuous filament reinforcement grade glass fibres are converted into a variety of different materials for the production of

TABLE I   PROPERTIES OF DIFFERENT GLASSES

| Property | Type of Glass | | | | | High Modulus |
	E	A	C	S	R	
S.G.	2.56	2.45	2.45	2.49	2.58	2.89
Tensile strength						
GN/m²	3.6	3.3	—	4.5	4.4	3.4
lb/in²x10³	540	495	—	675	660	510
Youngs Modulus						
GN/m²	75.9	69.0	—	86.2	84.8	110.4
lb/in²x10⁶	11.4	10.35	—	12.9	12.7	16.6
Softening						
point °C	850	700	690	—	990	—

GRP mouldings, etc. The most common form is chopped strand mats produced by chopping continuous filaments into lengths of about 2in (50mm) which are drawn down a hood to build up a loose mat form on a moving, open mesh conveyor. Binders are applied to hold the strands together and, after heating, the mat is compressed slightly and the bonded product is wound into rolls. Two principal binders are in use: powder and emulsion. Internationally, a polyester powder is the most widely used binder. When heated, this sticks the mat together where the glass strands cross each other. Powder-bonded mat is used for all types of moulding throughout the world.

The other type of binder is polyvinyl acetate emulsion used to coat each strand completely and again to stick the mat together. This type of binder has the particular advantage of dissolving rapidly in resin. Thus emulsion or 'liquid' bonded mats can be moulded much more easily into complicated shapes, compared with powder binder mats. In addition the form of the mat can also be varied to provide faster, easier wet cut, or controlled wet-cut, as required. For specialised applications it is well worth looking into the various types of emulsion-bonded chopped strand mats available.

Chopped Strands

Chopped Strands are also used on their own, particularly for producing polyester and alkyd moulding compounds for hot press mouldings and also for reinforcement of injection-moulded thermoplastics. Length of chopped strands available ranges from a minimum of about $\frac{1}{8}$in (3mm) to 2in (50mm). The sizing of the fibres together with the length and diameter of the strands can be selected to provide high strand integrity, low filamentation and compatibility with different polymers. Again, therefore, there is a choice of chopped strand material available for specific purposes.

Yarn

Yarns are produced from continuous filament by a twisting process which puts from 20 to 40 turns per metre into strand before being wound on to bobbins for weaving etc. *Plied* yarns are produced by twisting several single yarns together.

Rovings

Rovings take the form of cylindrical 'packages' wound from several strands of reinforcement gathered into a bundle with no twist. They are used for weaving cloths, for filament wound GRP mouldings, and as *chopping* rovings for 'gun' applications with hand or mechanical chopping process. *Chopped* rovings are also used in the production of dough moulding compounds (DMC) and bulk moulding compounds (BMC).

Reinforcement Fabrics

Woven fabrics have higher strength than mats as reinforcement materials, but one of their chief advantages is consistency of form (e.g. uniform thickness and weight). They are produced from yarn (woven glass cloth) and rovings (woven rovings).

Woven glass cloths. These generally produce the strongest laminates, but are not always easy to wet out thoroughly. The greatest tensile strength is obtained by using the thinnest cloths with the closest weave, which can aggravate this particular problem. As a consequence, interlaminar adhesion can be poor locally. Inter-layer bonding is usually improved by using thicker cloths and fewer layers.

Woven roving. These cloths are obtainable in various thicknesses – e.g. in weights from about 1 ounce per sq. ft. ($300/m^2$) upwards. They do not have the same strength as woven cloths but drape well and wet out fairly easily. Since they cost less than woven cloths they are often used as a reinforcement layer or layers in conjunction with glass fibre mat, or as a simple means of adding bulk to increase stiffness.

Rovings. These again are normally used for reinforcing glass mat layers, and also to add bulk and improve stiffness. They are widely used for strength purposes in boat hull construction.

For many applications a heavy fabric made from rovings is a preferred choice because it is the least compacted form of woven glass fibre, wets out more quickly and picks up far less resin than other fabric materials.

Weaves and Constructions

The construction of a woven fabric can be varied to provide particular characteristics required from the reinforcement material. Tensile strength can be balanced in all directions, or given a maximum value in a particular direction by suitable arrangement of warp and weft directions. The type of weave also largely governs the drape characteristics of the fabric as well as affecting the ease of wetting out.

The main types of weaves used are:–

Plain weave (Fig. 3.1) – having a simple structure in which each warp and weft yarn passes over one end or pick and under the next. This construction gives a reinforcement fabric that is widely used in general applications and can be relied upon to give reproducible laminate thickness. Tightly woven plain weave fabrics are sometimes difficult to wet out quickly.

Twill Weave (Fig. 3.2) – in which the number of warp ends and weft picks which pass over each other can be varied to give twills of various constructions, such as the 2x1 example shown. The diagram shows how the weft yarn passes under two warp ends and then over one warp end. The interlacing is arranged regularly forming a distinct diagonal line on the cloth surface.

FIG. 3.1

Drawing, to much enlarged scale, of plain weave, strands alternately crossing over and under.

FIG. 3.2

Drawing of twill weave in woven cloth for general purpose use.

FIG. 3.3

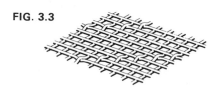

Drawing of satin weave. Satin weave produces a smooth cloth.

FIG. 3.4

Undirectional weave where the cloth is appreciably stronger in one 'preferred' direction.

Twills will follow contours more easily than plain fabrics and are much easier to wet out.

Satin Weave (Fig. 3.3)—similar to twills but the number of ends and picks which pass over each other before interlacing is greater. The interlacing is always with one crossing thread so that one side of the fabric is comprised mainly of warp yarns and the other of weft yarns. Among the several characteristics that make satins eminently suitable as reinforcement fabrics are: excellent drapeability, smooth surface, minimum thickness, high tensile and flexural strengths.

Matt Weave—have two or more threads woven as a single thread in both directions and can be produced in plain, twill, satin and other weaves.

Unidirectional Construction (Fig. 3.4)—which gives a fabric with its mechanical properties most favourable in one direction. The fabric may be of plain, satin, or any other weave.

In addition various hybrid constructions are produced for special applications, or to provide a glassfibre product competitive with cotton fibre or aramid fibre reinforcements.

In catalogues of materials intended for amateur GRP work, the type of weave is seldom specified—or referred to generally as 'close weave' and 'open weave'. The former defines a general purpose cloth for reinforcement purposes, or patching. Thin (i.e. light weight) open weave cloth is generally known as *scrim*.

Pre-treatment of Cloths

Woven glass fabrics are normally cleaned as part of their manufacturing process, either by batch heat treatment or caramalising. This type of finish is known as BHC Standard or BHC and can be regarded as a general purpose finish suitable for most applications.

For higher quality work, woven glass fabrics may be chemically treated to enhance their wetting out properties with resin. Examples of treatment are:

Amino silane or epoxy silane—particularly if the fabric is to be used with an epoxy laminating resin.

Methacrylate chromic chloride (Volan)—producing superior bonding with polyester resins.

Epoxy silane—giving the best bond of all with polyester resins.

Vinyl silane—producing a better bond with polyester resins than BHC finish.

Fabmat

Fabmat is the name of glass reinforcement material consisting of one layer of woven roving mat bonded to one layer of chopped strand mat. It is available in various weights specified by two numbers designating the weight of woven roving mat and CSM, respectively—e.g. 800/400 is $800g/m^2$ woven roving mat bonded to $400g/m^2$ CSM. The glass weight is thus the sum of the two—i.e. in this case $1200g/m^2$ or $4oz/ft^2$.

Whilst a very useful material for large mouldings, Fabmat is difficult to handle if cut up into small pieces because it then tends to break up or fall apart.

Glass Fibre Tissue

Glass fibre tissue or *surfacing tissue* was originally developed to hide the pattern of glass cloths when laid up in matched metal moulds, and also to be used as a 'cushioning' layer between the gel coat and the main reinforcement layers in any moulding or lay-up produced in a female mould. For general use it has two main applications:–

(a) As a finishing layer on a chopped strand mat lay-up to cover up the coarse glass pattern of the mat before adding a final gel coat.

(b) As a finish applied over a set gel coat. Again this will prevent any glass pattern appearing in the finished surface, and it also provides some reinforcement for the gel coat.

Modern surfacing tissues are produced in 0.25mm (.01in) and 0.4mm (.016in) thickness from chemically resistant glass giving maximum resistance to both acids and alkalis. The thicker tissue gives a better surface finish in laminates with a heavy fibre pattern and also has better weathering properties.

Another form of surface tissue known as *overlay veil* is produced specifically for use in closed mould processes and has special crease resistant properties. It would not normally be used for hand lay-up moulding, largely because of its low binder content (4% as against 7-11% in surfacing tissues).

A styrene binder is used with glass fibre tissues, being highly soluble in polyester resins.

Glass Fibre Tape

This is simply woven cloth in tape form, and is the most convenient material to use where narrow strips of reinforcement are required for spiral bindings. It is a strong material, readily handled, and easy to use for small repair jobs, etc. Tape is correctly specified by width and thickness.

Pre-impregnated Glass Fibre

Glass fibre cloth and mat are also produced uniformly impregnated with a resin-catalyst mix which can be activated by heat. In other words, the material is complete in itself for lay-up work which can be cured by heat and pressure. In its original state the material is slightly tacky, which can help in laying up. It is, however, only used for hot press mouldings and generally unsuitable for amateur work because both heat and pressure are required to cure. Pre-impregnated glass fibre is known variously as 'pre-preg', sheet moulding material, etc.

Sheet Moulding Compounds (SMC)

Sheet moulding compound (SMC) consists of a mixture of chopped strand mat or chopped rovings with resin, filler, catalyst and pigment in the form of a pliable sheet. It is used for hot press moulding only, the material flowing and curing under pressure and heat.

Dough Moulding Compounds

Dough Moulding Compound (DMC) and Bulk Moulding Compound (BMC) consists of a mixture of chopped strands, resin, filler, catalyst and pigment, usually supplied in the form of a dough or rope.

Table II is a general selection guide to the type of glass fibre reinforcement used for particular applications.

The Alternatives

Three other materials are used as alternative reinforcement materials to glass fibre—aramid fibre, carbon fibre and polyester fibre. All three are used in woven fabric form, although carbon fibre is also used in the form of bundles or 'tows' of plain filaments.

Aramid Fibre (Kevlar)

Kevlar or aramid fibre is fundamentally a type of nylon. It has become a direct alternative to glass fibre for laminates requiring high strength with lower weight. It is much more costly than glass fibre reinforcement, however, and only available in woven roving tape form. The type specially finished for optimum bonding characteristics with epoxy resin is known as *Kevlar 49*. This is also suitable for use with polyester resins, but again for optimum bond should have a finish specially formulated *for* use with polyester resins.

As far as simple comparisons go, a laminate made with Kevlar is thicker (and stronger) than GRP for the same weight, and also appreciably stiffer. This means that a laminate can be made as strong and stiff as GRP but at reduced weight—a weight saving of as much as 30-40% is possible in some cases. Where Kevlar does compare poorly, however, is in *compressive* strength, which is substantially lower than GRP. Thus whilst a Kevlar laminate can save weight and still give the same (or better) *tensile* strength and resistance to impact as GRP it has less flexural strength to resist *buckling* loads. Nevertheless it is probably the best material to consider where weight saving is important since it can be used for lay-up work in just the same way as glass reinforcement.

There are differences here, though. For a start Kevlar is much more difficult to cut—it needs a *very* sharp knife—and cutting or trimming a cured moulding is more difficult. Another difference when Kevlar is being used in a lay-up is that it does not change its appearance and become translucent like glass reinforcement when wetted with resin. This can give the impression that the laminate is too dry, when the natural reaction is to apply more resin. The end result could be a Kevlar laminate with an excess of resin which may now weigh as much as the GRP counterpart. The answer to this particular problem

TABLE II   LAMINATE TYPES FOR HAND LAY-UP

	Laminate type	Remarks
	(i) gel coat (ii) chopped strand mat	Typical general purpose laminate for all types of mouldings. CSM thickness (weight) as required for strength.
	(i) gel coat (ii) surfacing tissue (iii) chopped strand mat	All types of laminates where superior surface finish is required.
	(i) gel coat (ii) surfacing tissue (iii) chopped strand mat (iv) surfacing tissue (v) 'inside' gel coat	All types of laminates where best surface finish is required on both sides of moulding. Layer (v) may be omitted, or used as an alternative to (iv).
	(i) gel coat (ii) surfacing tissue (iii) chopped strand mat (iv) woven roving (v) chopped strand mat	Mouldings requiring superior strength. Incorporate as many alternating layers of CSM and rovings as necessary. Layer (ii) may be omitted.
	(i) gel coat (ii) surfacing tissue (iii) chopped strand mat (iv) woven fabric (v) chopped strand mat	Not recommended but may be used for higher strength mouldings incorporating as many alternating layers of CSM and cloth as necessary.
	(i) gel coat (ii) surfacing tissue (iii) woven fabric (iv) woven fabric	Not recommended. Layers of woven fabric, where used, should be alternated with CSM.

is to use only the specified quantity of resin required for the laminate and *not* to exceed this.

The other problem posed by the consistent opaqueness of Kevlar is that trapped air bubbles are not easily seen, as with glass. For this reason it is *essential* that a Kevlar laminate be really well rollered to consolidate.

Kevlar is also rather less tolerant as regards polyester resins than glass fibre, although the finishes now used on Kevlar 49 have minimised this particular problem with resulting improvements in flexural strength and shear strength in finished laminates. Isophthalic polyester resins give the best laminates with Kevlar, although a further improvement can be obtained using vinylester resins. The best resin of all for Kevlar laminates is epoxy, although this is too expensive for large scale use. They could be well worth the extra cost in model projects—e.g. producing a fuselage moulding or a racing powerboat hull moulding appreciably lighter than a GRP moulding for the same overall strength.

Carbon Fibre

Carbon fibre started as an aerospace material, offering exceptional strength with light weight when used as a resin reinforcement. It is expensive and not easy to obtain in small quantities in either woven or tow form, so its application is somewhat limited outside specialised productions.

Carbon fibres are produced in two forms—*high strength* (HS) and *high modulus* (HM). Both give laminates with high strength, good fatigue and vibration resistance, low friction, and good resistance to wear. Carbon fibre, in fact, produces laminates or reinforced mouldings of the highest strength and best strength/weight ratio of all the reinforcement materials.

Polyester Fibre

Fabrics woven from *polyester fibre* are also used for laminates requiring high impact resistance. It is the best material of all in this respect, and also the lightest of the reinforcing materials. On the other hand it is basically a 'limp' material and polyester reinforced plastic laminates lack stiffness. It is thus not suitable for mouldings which need to be rigid.

Comparative properties of the various fibre reinforcement materials are summarised in Table III.

TABLE III   PROPERTIES OF FIBRE REINFORCEMENT MATERIALS

Material	Specific Gravity	Tensile Strength N/m² lb/m²		Tensile Modulus N/m² lb/m²		Specific Tensile Strength N/m² lb/m²		Specific Tensile Modulus N/m² lb/m²	
E-glass	2.56	3.4	4.9×10^5	72	10×10^6	1.34	1.9×10^5	28	4×10^6
S-glass	2.50	4.0	5.8×10^5	86	12.5×10^6	1.57	2.3×10^5	34	5×10^6
Kevlar 49	1.45	3.6	5.2×10^5	130	18.9×10^6	2.48	3.6×10^5	90	13×10^6
Carbon HS	1.74	3.1	4.5×10^5	227	33×10^6	1.77	2.6×10^5	130	19×10^6
Carbon HM	1.81	2.1	3×10^5	390	56×10^6	1.16	1.7×10^5	215	31×10^6
Polyester	1.38	1.0	1.5×10^5	11	1.6×10^6	0.72	1.0×10^5	8	1×10^6

Note:
Tensile strength is a direct measure of the resistance of the material to breaking when subject to a stretching load. The highest value in this column thus represents the strongest material, and pro rata.
Specific Tensile strength is a measure of the tensile strength/weight ratio. Figures in this column are thus a direct measure of the strength/weight ratio of the materials.
Tensile Modulus can be read as a measure of the 'stiffness' of the material. The higher the figure in this column the stronger and stiffer the reinforcement properties.
Specific Tensile Modulus is a measure of the 'stiffness'/weight ratio. The higher the figure in this column the better the performance as a lightweight reinforcement.

CHAPTER FOUR

Resins

By far the majority of GRP mouldings are produced using unsaturated *polyester resins.* 'Unsaturated' means that the resin is capable of being 'cured' from a liquid to a solid state, this being brought about by dissolving the polyester in a suitable monomer, usually styrene. A polyester resin of this type can be made to set in the form of a hard and permanent solid by the addition of a catalyst, and satisfactorily moulded without the use of pressure. In this state the resin is said to be cured, or polymerised.

Curing with just the addition of a catalyst also requires heat to complete the process. However, the resin can be made to set at room temperatures, or 'cold cure', by the further addition of an accelerator. This is obviously preferable, for it considerably simplifies the process. The two types of cure are essentially the same. With cold curing, heat is actually produced exothermically (or internally, as far as the resin is concerned), and so the end result is exactly the same. Resin plus catalyst, hot cured has the same characteristics as resin plus catalyst plus accelerator, cold-cured.

A polyester resin is not a single material. There are many different types of these resins, each with different characteristics. These may range from strong, hard solids when cured, to quite flexible materials. The majority are formulated for GRP lay-up work. Others are specially formulated for casting, surface coatings, stopper compounds, nut locking or thread sealants,

and even as a mortar for concrete constructions. All are unsaturated resins, capable of being cured. *Saturated* polyesters are quite a different material, and cannot be cured in the same way–e.g. Terylene is a saturated polyester.

Alternative Resins

While the wide range of different polyester resins available covers the requirements of most GRP mouldings, other resins may be used for particular application (e.g. for better resistance to attack by certain chemicals). These are:–

(i) *Epoxide resins* (or epoxy resins) – which are a typical alternative choice where polyester resins may not show all the properties required. They are, however, appreciably more expensive than polyester resins.

(ii) *Furane resins*–which are produced by the self-condensation of furfurol with furfurol alcohol have even better resistance to certain chemicals than epoxy.

(iii) *Silicone resins*–again an expensive type, also with less strength than polyester or epoxy resins but capable of withstanding higher temperatures without degradation. Also silicone resins do not burn. They have very limited applications, however, and are little used except for very specialised applications.

(iv) *Phenolic resins*–which are produced

by condensing phenol with formaldehyde. Again these have only specialised applications and until recently such moulding resins were only available in powder form for use with compression moulding techniques. Some liquid types are now available, however, which are suitable for hand lay-up mouldings.

Polyester Resins for General Work

As far as the amateur and semi-professional worker is concerned, all his requirements will normally be met by a suitable choice of *polyester resin*. The choice is very wide indeed. Table IV, for example, summarises the product range of one manufacturer (see also Appendix 8). At the other end of the scale, the range generally available and widely obtainable for small-quantity amateur use is normally restricted to a few types known, typically, as *gel coat resins* and *general purpose resins*.

Gel Coat Resins

Gel coat resins are formulated in a different way from resins used for laminating. They need to be an air-inhibited type (see later) which sets rapidly on the surface in contact with the mould but remains tacky on the other side of the film whilst still exposed to air. This ensures a good bond to the first layer of laminate when applied. They also need to dry with a high gloss and a certain degree of resilience and provide a thin surface layer which will not readily crack or deteriorate—properties which have to be provided by the resin itself since the gel coat contains no reinforcement. The resin gel is also the one layer in which coloured pigments (and sometimes also filler) are incorporated to produce a moulding with self-colour.

As a basic rule, therefore, *only a gel coat resin should be used for the initial gel coat.* A laminating resin or general purpose resin is *not* suitable. However, this latter type of resin is suitable for producing a final gel coat over the *last* layer of the laminate, if required, whereas a true gel coat resin would not be (it would tend to remain sticky on the final surface exposed to air). Almost all gel coat resins are *pre-accelerated* (i.e. are formulated so that they will resist running or sagging, like thixotropic paint). It may also be ready *pigmented*. White pigmented gel coat resins are readily available; for other colours the pigment is normally added to a 'plain' gel coat resin (which may, in fact, be slightly pinkish in colour).

An important point in selecting a gel coat resin is that different formulations are used for resins prepared for *brush* application, or *spraying* on. Brushing gel coat resins are thicker (more viscous) and not generally suitable for spraying. Mixing them with thinners to make them easily sprayable can seriously degrade their properties as a gel coat resin. So, for spray application, use a gel coat resin already formulated *for* spraying.

Gel coat resins may also be of a specific type—e.g. *flexible* to resist deformation without cracking; *rigid* to produce a hard glassfibre surface on a rigid moulding; *fire-retardant;* or *chemically resistant.*

General Purpose Resins

A *general purpose resin* is the common type of laminating resin, also the lowest in cost. It is suitable for all types of GRP work and is most widely supplied in pre-accelerated form, with a standard catalyst. An additional catalyst may also be available to produce more rapid hardening at low temperatures. This is normally called a 'winter additive' or similar, and is added to the main catalyst in specific proportions when necessary.

Resins with enhanced storage life, or intended for storage in warm climates, normally have the accelerator omitted.

Actually the number of resins which qualify as 'general purpose' is quite wide and may range from those with only moderate (or even inferior) properties to high quality types with excellent water, chemical and weathering resistance. The latter may be described as *marine* or *boatbuilding* resins, or *high-duty* resins. Price can range up to twice that of an ordinary general performance resin or more.

Fire-Retardant Resins

The description *fire-retardant* is sometimes given to resins specially formulated to improve resistance to flame, or give it self-extinguishing properties. A more accurate description is *reduced-flammability resin* since such resins are not 'fireproof' as such. Basically they provide a low fire hazard whereas an ordinary polyester resin will burn freely once ignited.

Chemically Resistant Resins

Special chemically resistant polyester resins are formulated to provide enhanced resistance to mineral acids, inorganic salts, fats, oils, etc. at moderate temperatures. They can also offer advantages for mouldings used in contact with foodstuffs, although no more free from tainting than an ordinary polyester resin until the full styrene content has been leached out of the finished moulding (see also Appendix 4).

Reduced Styrene Emission Resins

These are general purpose resins formulated with additives to give substantially reduced styrene volatilisation during lamination—also called *environmental resins* because of the improved working atmosphere resulting. Otherwise they are identical to general purpose resins. In fact, all general purpose resins now produced by at least one major manufacturer are environmental resins.

Thixotropic Resins

Thixotropic or 'non-sag' resins may be of various types, the main feature being the incorporation of an additive which prevents the resin running and thus draining off vertical surfaces in a lay-up. Ordinary resins can also be made 'non-running' by the addition of thixotropic agents.

Non-thixotropic Resins

Non-thixotropic resins are used for particular applications where the property of the resin being free to 'run' is an advantage—e.g. the production of castings, or for flow coatings used in certain commercial productions.

Casting Resin

These are specially formulated for casting work. Their properties are 'tailored' to the characteristics required, e.g. good optical properties for resins used for decorative work or embedding botanical or zoological specimens, good dielectric properties for resins used to encapsulate electronic components. Low volumetric shrinkage is also important in a casting resin.

Flexible Resins

These are used for blending with a more rigid resin to vary the 'elastic' properties, and thus control the resilience of the finished GRP moulding.

Plasticised Resins

These are softened resins, produced by the addition of a plasticising agent such as dimethyl phthalate. Again these impart flexibility to the resin, but are employed only in special circumstances. These include the formulation of resins as thread locking compounds, and resins for the production of large castings. Plasticised resins should never normally be used for introducing resilience into GRP mouldings as there is always the distinct possibility of the plastic leaching out.

Clear Resins

These are also known as 'rooflite' resins, translucent resins, etc., and are light-stabilised resins, intended for use in the production of translucent rooflight sheeting, decorative panels, etc. They are formulated to give optimum optical properties with freedom from discoloration with age, i.e. are particularly resistant to ultra violet light. All normal GRP mouldings will tend to yellow slightly with age, although this effect is not usually very noticeable except on translucent products.

'Rapid' Resins

These are pre-accelerated resins where the accelerator used, and matching catalyst, produce fast gel and hardening times. They are intended mainly for emergency repair work, but can also be used for general work in colder weather provided the mouldings involved are not too large.

One-Component Resins

One-component resins which require no hardener and cold-cure by exposure to light are quite new. Known also as *one-pot resin,* the resin is used straight from the pot and hardens by the amount of light is subsequently receives. This light can be ordinary daylight, or an electric bulb. An ordinary 150 watt bulb placed 10in (28cm) away from the surface will cure a 6in (15cm) diameter area in about 45 minutes; a 150 watt reflector bulb a larger area in the same time. Hardening in daylight will take somewhat longer, but covers the whole area exposed to daylight.

Apart from the obvious advantage of a one-pot resin being simpler to use, the other advantage is that areas of a laminate can be shielded from light to hold back the cure if advantageous. For example a certain area could be shielded so that it remains wet after the rest of the moulding has hardened, facilitating bonding on of other parts to that area.

Limitations of light-curing one-pot resins are that they are not suitable for use with heavily pigmented or filled resin, or with core materials or reinforcement materials such as Kevlar and carbon fibre due to lack of light penetration. Also, using light bulbs as a light source, care is necessary to avoid scorching or burning the laminate by building up excessive heat.

Resins of this type normally have a 'built-in' indicator of cure—i.e. they are originally coloured and gradually lose their colour as they cure. The disappearance of colour indicates that the resin has fully hardened. Equally, any loss of colour in unused one-pot resin indicates that it has started to harden.

Special Purpose Resins

Special-purpose resins are formulated to enhance specific properties and are not normally generally available. They are intended for commercial productions calling for properties not met by standard resins. Examples are resins produced specifically for moulding by resin injection or cold pressing processes.

For rather more technical explanations of polyester resins, see Appendix 8.

Inhibited and Non-Inhibited Resins

Most general purpose or lay-up resins contain a small amount of wax. This is not enough to have any inhibiting effect on the resin and, during curing, the wax migrates to the surface to speed formation of a tack-free surface. Such resins are referred to as non air inhibited types. Those which have only a very small proportion of wax (0.02% or less) are called *partially non air inhibited resins* and set with a high surface gloss. Those with a higher wax content (0.06%) are wholly *non air inhibited resins* with even greater surface hardening and a non-gloss appearance. Too much wax, however, can inhibit curing and lead to delamination.

By contrast gel coat resins (and certain other types) contain no wax at all and are termed *air-inhibited resins.*

The difference is basically this. An air-inhibited resin sets rapidly on the side from which air is excluded, i.e. on the side against the mould in the case of a gel coat. The other side, being in contact with air, continues to remain tacky for some considerable time. That means there is no immediate hurry to lay up the next layer of laminate, but as soon as this is done air is excluded from that side of the gel coat which now sets rapidly.

With a non air inhibited resin the *outer* surface exposed to air tends to harden rapidly, so succeeding layers must be applied reasonably soon. On the other hand, after completing the lay-up of the final layer the exposed surface of the resin hardens quickly and should become tack free in a short time, like a gel coat the other way round.

If the resin used for lay-up is an air-inhibited type the inside surface of a finished lay-up may tend to remain tacky for a long time, although the laminate itself has set hard. To make this tackiness disappear quickly (i.e. to harden the surface rapidly), air must be *excluded* from it. This can be done by covering the surface with a sheet of polythene pressed down in intimate contact with the whole surface, or painting with release agent. In the later case, the release agent should be washed off after about 24 hours.

In some types of resin, air-inhibiting or non air-inhibiting characteristics are given by chemical additives rather than wax—e.g. particularly in the case of fire retardant resins and acid-resistant resins.

Resin Life

Resins are best when fresh, so as far as possible should be bought from a source which has a good turnover of supplies. Normally manufacturers guarantee resins for two months, but they will keep much longer if stored in a cool dark place. Basically a resin is still usable as long as it is still liquid, but if too old can develop jelly-like lumps. In this state it is not usable (unless the lumps are filtered out) because it will not brush out or even roll out properly in a lay-up, leaving inconsistent patches where the lumps are.

Most resins are premixed with accelerator. During long storage the accelerator content can separate out into particles

TABLE IV BEETLE* POLYESTER RESINS FOR HAND LAY-UP

	Resin No.	Viscosity	Pre-accelerated	Gel Time at 20°C	Cure System	Barcol Hardness	Lloyds Approval	Remarks
Gel Coat	8181	HIGH-THIX	✓	15	2% MRKP	40	✓	Isophthalic resin with good flexibility
	8182	HIGH-THIX	✓	15	2% MRKP	40	✓	White pigmented version of 8181
	8183	HIGH-THIX	✓	15	2% MRKP	50		Specially suitable for mould making
	8185	HIGH-THIX	✓	15	2% MRKP	50		Meets BS 476
	8187	HIGH-THIX	✓	9	2% MRKP	40	✓	Spray version of 8181
	8188	HIGH-THIX	✓	9	2% MRKP	40	✓	Spray version of 8182
General purpose	837E	LOW-THIX	✓	16	1% MRKP	50	✓	Very fast gel and cure
	840E	LOW-THIX	✓	30	2% MRKP	50	✓	Medium cure rate for larger mouldings
	864E	LOW-THIX	✓	23	2% MRKP	50	✓	Fast gel and cure
	865E	LOW-THIX	✓	23	2% MRKP	50	✓	Suitable for spraying
	876E	LOW-THIX	✓	21	2% MRKP 1% COBALT	50	✓	Formulated for marine applications
	888E	LOW-THIX	✓	30	2% MRKP	50	✓	Long pot life with rapid cure
	889E	LOW-THIX	✓	30	2% MRKP	50	✓	White pigmented version of 888E
Fire retardant	849	LOW-THIX	✓	23	2% MRKP	50	—	Reduced flammability
	855	MED-THIX	✓	17	2% MRKP	55	—	resins conforming
	856	LOW-THIX	✓	24	2% MRKP 1% COBALT	45	—	to BS 476 in
	879	HIGH-THIX	✓	23	2% MRKP	40	—	various categories
	896	LOW-THIX	✓	15	2% MRKP	50	—	
Chemical resist	844	HIGH-THIX		27	3% BENZOYL	35	—	Biphenol resin for aggressive environments
	870	LOW-THIX		33	2% MRKP 1% COBALT	50	—	HET-acid resin for high temps.
	846	MED-THIX		26	2% MRKP 1% COBALT	45	—	Isophthalic resin for less aggressive environ.
	874	MED-THIX		20	2% MRKP 1% COBALT	50	—	High reactivity. Also for mould making
	838	MED-THIX		36	2% MRKP 1% COBALT	45	✓	Isophthalic laminating resin for marine applications

*British Industrial Plastics Limited

Glass % by weight

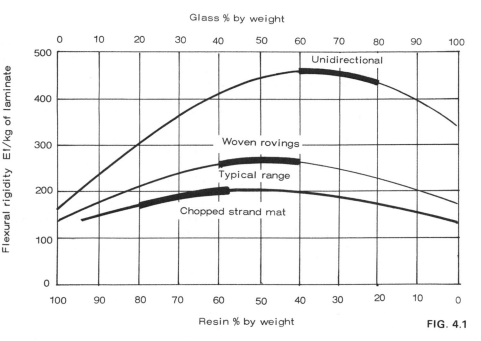

FIG. 4.1

which 'drift' to the bottom of the resin. This leaves the upper part of the resin starved of accelerator, while the higher concentration at the bottom provides gradual hardening of the resin from the bottom upwards. Provided the bottom resin has not gelled it is still usable, but additional accelerator may need to be added to the bulk of the resin.

Catalyst Life

Catalysts also deteriorate with age. The onset of deterioration is shown by 'gassing', when the catalyst starts to lose its peroxide content. At the same time the catalyst will start to discolour.

Manufacturers normally guarantee a minimum life of six months for catalysts, but in practice they will keep for very much longer if stored in a cool, dark place. Stored

in a warm atmosphere a catalyst will deteriorate much more rapidly. Rapid deterioration can also occur (detected by discoloration) if the catalyst becomes contaminated. Stored in glass bottles or clear containers and exposed to strong sunlight, catalysts can decompose very rapidly and even self-ignite or explode.

Resin to Glass Ratio

As a rough rule for producing hand lay-up laminates in chopped strand mat the amount of resin necessary to achieve proper wetting out and consolidation of the laminate will be $2\frac{1}{2}$ times the total glass weight, regardless of the actual number of *layers* or total *thickness* of glass used. This applies particularly when using a *roller* to consolidate the laminate. Using a brush to apply the resin and 'stipple' the glass down, a resin weight of anything up to 4 times the total glass weight may be required. Not all this resin will necessarily be incorporated in the laminate—some will inevitably be wasted—but it will be more difficult to control the final amount of resin used in the laminate or the final resin to glass ratio.

With woven glass cloth and rovings the amount of resin used is normally the *same* weight as that of the glass—i.e. a 1:1 resin-to-glass ratio. Again, however, much more resin could be used with brush working rather than rollering, i.e. increasing the resin-to-glass ratio.

These are only general figures, applicable to average workmanship. It is possible to reduce the amount of resin and obtain a higher glass:resin ratio (which is favourable to strength) if particular care is taken to ensure that each glass layer is thoroughly wetted with resin during the lay-up. Equally, it is possible to use more resin, which will make it easier to ensure complete wetting out, but reduces the glass:resin ratio and the strength of the moulding. In the case of glass cloth reinforcement, which is more difficult to wet out, actual resin:glass ratios may be even more variable, depending on the type of cloth used, and individual technique.

More Precise Figures

Theoretically, at least, glass fibre being stronger than resin, the *lower* the resin to glass ratio the better. In practice, however, this mainly refers to *tensile* strength of the finished laminate. The amount of *flexural rigidity* in the finished laminate is far from critical as regards resin to glass ratio, as shown in Fig. 4.1. Thus in the case of chopped strand mat there is relatively *little* variation in flexural strength with resin to glass ratio, with a normal optimum of 60% (resin:glass). Similarly for woven rovings which have a nominal maximum flexural strength of 1:1 resin:glass ratio. With woven materials having uni-directional mechanical properties, however, the optimum performance range is more marked—i.e. normally between 60 and 30% resin:glass ratios with a maximum at about 40% resin:glass.

Another way to look at resin to glass ratios is in terms of total cost, again specifically applied to flexural strength. The more nearly the cost of *resin* approaches the cost of *glass reinforcement* the less critical the choice of resin to glass ratio becomes in terms of flexural strength per £ total cost. In fact the most cost effective material in this respect is chopped strand mat and the least cost effective is woven roving.

In the case of chopped strand mat, if the cost per weight of this is the same as that of resin, then the *cost* of achieving a certain flexural rigidity in a given laminate is *independent* of the resin to glass ratio. It does not matter what resin to glass ratio you use within the limits of actual lay-up requirements, i.e. you must have enough resin to wet out the glass thoroughly. With hand lay-up this will normally take at least twice the amount of resin than glass (i.e. minimum resin to glass ratio of 2:1).

With chopped strand mat laminates, therefore, there is no particular need to worry too much about resin to glass ratios actually achieved. (See also Appendix 1, 2 and 3).

CHAPTER FIVE

Accelerators, catalysts and curing

Pre-accelerated resins are normally the most convenient to use since the accelerator proportions are already adjusted to give the most suitable gelling and hardening characteristics, once the catalyst is added to start the curing reaction at room temperature. If a 'straight' resin is used, the accelerator and catalyst must be added separately, the order of mixing depending on the particular application involved.

With a pre-accelerated resin, addition of the catalyst (or *hardener,* as it is often called) will immediately start the cold-curing process, causing the resin to thicken and gel, and finally set hard. The resin has a usable pot life over the period during which it is thickening, but still remains workable. The gel time is governed mainly by the amount of *accelerator* present. The less the accelerator the longer the gel time. Cutting down the amount of catalyst will also increase the gel time, but here there is a danger of having insufficient catalyst present, which can lead to an undercured moulding. With a pre-accelerated resin, therefore, it is not advisable to try to control gel time by adjusting the amount of catalyst used, but work strictly to recommended proportions of catalyst. If faster, or slower, gel times are required, then a pre-accelerated resin giving these particular characteristics can be used.

There is, however, another way of adjusting the gel time. This is by using a different type of catalyst. Thus with a pre-accelerated resin the following alternatives

may be offered by various suppliers.

(i) Resins with different proportions of accelerator (or different accelerators) to give (a) normal gel times; (b) faster curing for colder weather use, or emergency repairs; (c) slower curing for increased pot life in hot weather. Catalyst proportions would be specific in each case.

(ii A single resin which can be used with different catalysts to give different gel and hardening times.

With a 'straight' resin, the choice of accelerator and catalyst is under the control of the user, who can thus adjust the mix to suit his particular requirements. However, in this case there is more chance of going wrong. The system is more flexible though, for there is the further choice of:—

(i) Mixing the *catalyst* with the resin first, which will give a pot life of some 20 hours or more under normal conditions, adding the accelerator in the proportion required for making up the mix for immediate use.

(ii) Mixing the *accelerator* with the resin, and adding the catalyst in the proportion required for immediate use. This is virtually the same as using a pre-accelerated resin, except that the user has control over the type and proportion of accelerator used.

It is important to note that *accelerator and catalyst should never be mixed together directly.* This could result in a violent, even explosive reaction. One or other must *always* be added *to the resin first.*

Accelerators

Quite a number of different chemical compounds are effective as accelerators in promoting cold-setting of polyester resins in the presence of a catalyst. Some have only a limited use (such as tin, vanadium and zirconium salts and certain ammonium compounds). Others are highly reactive, and normally used. These include metallic soaps (usually cobalt soap); and tertiary amines (such as dimethyl amine). There is probably not much to choose between the two types, except that an amine accelerator tends to produce a yellow discoloration in time. If the two types of accelerator are used together, however, much faster gelling and setting times can be realised. This method is used to produce a 'rapid' accelerator.

Catalysts (Hardener)

The catalysts used with polyester resins are almost invariably organic peroxides. These are unstable on their own—and can even explode. They are therefore normally supplied dispersed in a plasticiser in the form of a paste or a liquid, or in dry powder form mixed with an inert filler.

Catalysts should always be handled with care, especially if relatively large quantities are involved. They are all irritating to the skin and can cause burns unless washed off immediately. Injury can be more serious if catalyst is splashed into the eyes. Immediate treatment in such cases is to wash out the eyes continuously with plain water or weak bicarbonate solution.

Rags or waste used to mop up catalyst, or on which catalyst has been spilt, should be damped down with water and thrown

away in a dustbin. They should not be left lying around as they may self-ignite through spontaneous combustion.

The chief catalysts are:

(i) *Methyl-ethyl-ketone-peroxide* – which is probably the most reactive type, normally produced as a liquid.

(ii) *Cyclohexanone-peroxide*—which is less reactive, but more stable. It is normally prepared in paste form.

(iii) *Benzole-peroxide*—which is again very reactive and is normally available in either paste or powder form.

For amateur work a liquid catalyst (hardener) is generally preferred since it is easier to measure accurately, and disperse uniformly through the resin by stirring. Powdered catalysts, mixed with inert fillers, are used for fillers, mixes and body stoppers, in conjunction with a pre-accelerated resin (usually of the 'rapid' type).

Proportions

The setting action of the resin is initiated by the *catalyst* or hardener. The accelerator merely takes the place of heat—i.e. in the absence of the accelerator the catalysed resin can be cured by heat; or in the presence of accelerator the catalysed resin will cure at normal room temperature. The accelerator must, therefore, be present in sufficient quantity to activate the catalyst, if complete cold curing is to be produced in a short period of time. If there is a small deficiency of accelerator the gel time will be increased, while a larger deficiency of accelerator will result in undercuring, or very slow hardening. The proportion of accelerator, therefore, is not critical, provided there is enough. Usually this is between 1 and 4% of the resin weight, with the normal 'strength' of the accelerator as manufactured (e.g. typically a dilution

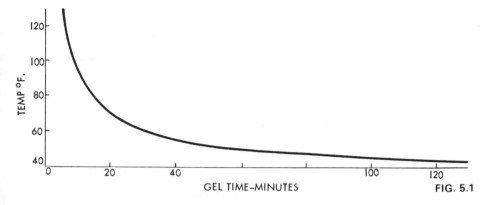

FIG. 5.1

giving 1% metal in the case of a cobalt soap).

Catalysts are usually formulated on a 25-50% peroxide 'strength', which yields a similar proportion requirement to the accelerator. Recommended proportions usually range between 1% and 4%, depending on the type of catalyst. From 1 to 2% will halve the gel time, but a further increase in catalyst will produce a more rapid increase in hardening. The gel time will not be greatly affected by increasing the catalyst above about 4% however, as shown in Fig. 5.1. Lack of catalyst, on the other hand, can lead to an incomplete cure.

The Cold-Curing Reaction

From the moment the catalyst is activated (either by heat or contact with the accelerator), the resin starts to set. Setting takes place over four definite stages:

1. *Pot life time*–during which the resin still remains in a workable liquid form although it is continuing to thicken.
2. *Gel time*–or the time taken for the resin to set to a soft gel.
3. *Hardening time*–which is the further time taken for the resin to become hard enough for the moulding to be removed from its mould.

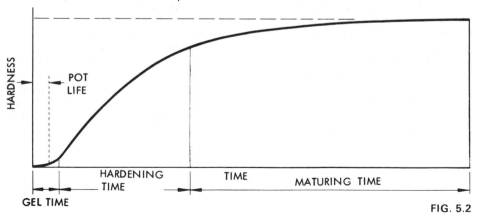

FIG. 5.2

31

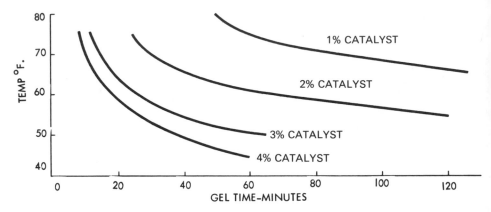

FIG. 5.3 GEL TIMES FOR A TYPICAL POLYESTER COLD-CURING RESIN

4. *Maturing time*–which is the further period of time over which the moulding will continue to gain hardness and, eventually, complete stability. When fully matured the moulding will have its maximum strength, hardness, chemical resistance and stability.

These four stages are illustrated in Fig. 5.2.

Pot life and gel time are strictly related to the activity of the catalyst. This is governed both by the proportion of the catalyst and the ambient temperature. For a given proportion of catalyst, the higher the air temperature the shorter will be the pot life and gel time of the resin, as shown in Fig. 5.3. This diagram shows the general effect of varying the proportion of catalyst to control the gel time at different ambient temperatures. These curves can only be used as a rough guide, however. They are specific to a particular resin-accelerator-catalyst combination. Most proprietary resin-hardener combinations do, however, give data on pot life and gel times for different temperatures, and details of how these can be adjusted, if necessary, or possible.

The *hardening time* can vary a lot

depending on the size and thickness of the moulding, and also the proportion of resin present. It will also again be affected by the air temperature. The warmer the air the more quickly the moulding will harden off. With a small moulding, and reasonably warm air, hardening time may only be an hour, or even less. With a large moulding it may need 12 or even 24 hours before the moulding is hard and rigid enough to be removed from its mould without fear of it sagging slightly, or becoming distorted in the process.

The majority of general purpose GRP mouldings can be considered suitable for use 24 hours after their hardening time has elapsed. Where the application is more critical, such as GRP boat hulls, water or petrol tanks, etc., or articles which must have good chemical resistance, a maturing time of several days, or even weeks may be necessary. It is recommended that a GRP fuel tank, for example, should be allowed a maturing time of at least one month, to be sure that the material will be fully stable when put into use.

For rather less critical applications, maturing time can be reduced to a matter of a few days by storing the moulding in a

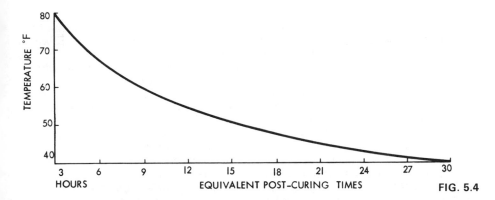

FIG. 5.4

warm atmosphere. Fig. 5.4. shows the effect of atmospheric temperature in terms of equivalent maturing times. Thus at a temperature of 80°C, for example, the maturing time is only one tenth that which would be necessary at 40°C. It is important not to try to accelerate maturing time with too much heat, however, and if a moulding is to be stored in a temperature much above 40°C it should first be allowed to mature naturally, at ordinary temperature, for 24 hours. If not, it may show signs of warping or distortion.

Some idea of the effect of maturing time on the properties of the GRP moulding can be obtained from Fig. 5.5 which shows how resistance to water and actual hardness improve with age.

The Exothermic Effect

It has already been mentioned that the cold-setting of the resin does, in fact, produce heat. This heating, which causes a rise in temperature in the GRP, does not take place until the resin has passed the gel

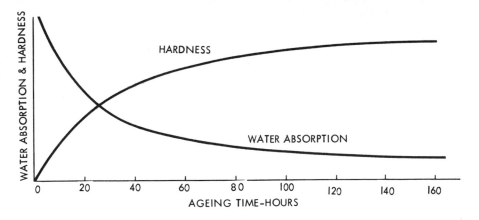

FIG. 5.5 EFFECT OF MATURING RESIN

33

state and is almost set—see Fig. 5.6. This effect is not normally noticeable, or significant, with the usual run of GRP work, but it can be important where a large bulk of resin is involved, such as in thick mouldings. To avoid excessive heating which could expand and distort the mould itself, it may be necessary to apply water cooling to the mould in such cases, or stop the lay-up after several layers of reinforcement have been added and let these harden before proceeding with the lay-up.

What will be noticed with ordinary mouldings is that the thicker the section the more rapid the hardening period is likely to be, because of the internal heat developed. Castings may need special care in order to ensure that the actual temperature of the set resin does not reach levels which could be damaging to objects which are being encapsulated (see Chapter 13).

Getting the Proportions Right

The majority of amateur constructions are done with pre-accelerated resins, leaving only the catalyst (hardener) to be added in recommended proportions. These pro-portions may range from 1 to 4%. These proportions can be read as the *weight* of catalyst (hardener) required to mix with a given *weight* of resin. Where the catalyst is a liquid or paste, this involves translating weight into terms of liquid measure.

Where small quantities of resin are involved, the catalyst (hardener) can be added by drop, using the following count:

5 drops equals 1% catalyst (hardener) per 1 ounce of resin

10 drops equals 2% catalyst (hardener) per 1 ounce of resin

15drops equals 3% catalyst (hardener) per 1 ounce of resin

20 drops equals 4% catalyst (hardener) per 1 ounce of resin

This still requires knowing the *weight* of resin to be used, but the proportion of resin required to match a particular glass fibre reinforcement can only be accurately determined by *weight* (see Chapter 7). You must, therefore, also have facilities for weighing.

For example, if the job calls for 2 ounces of resin, this can only be measured out by weighing an empty glass jar or similar container and then pouring resin into this container until the weight indicated has increased by 2 ounces. Alternatively you

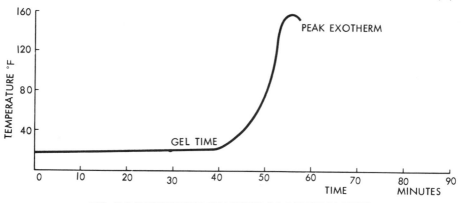

FIG. 5.6 EXOTHERMIC FRACTION OF A TYPICAL RESIN

TABLE V PROPORTIONS
(weight in ounces, except where noted)

Weight of Resin	% Catalyst or Accelerator			
	1	2	3	4
2 oz	10 drops	20 drops	30 drops	40 drops
4 oz	20 drops	40 drops	60 drops	0.16 ($\frac{1}{6}$)
8 oz	40 drops	0.16 ($\frac{1}{6}$)	$\frac{1}{4}$	0.32 ($\frac{1}{3}$)
1 lb	0.16 ($\frac{1}{6}$)	0.32 ($\frac{1}{3}$)	$\frac{1}{2}$	0.64 ($\frac{2}{3}$)
2 lb	0.32 ($\frac{1}{3}$)	0.64 ($\frac{2}{3}$)	1	1.3
5 lb	0.64 ($\frac{2}{3}$)	1.3	$2\frac{1}{2}$	3.2
10 lb	1.3	3.2	5	6.4

may be able to buy graduated measures (or one may be supplied with the resin), which shows the amount (volume) of resin to be poured in to make a certain weight.

Having obtained the 2 ounce measure of resin, the mix is to be prepared by adding, say 3% catalyst (hardener). Now 3% is 15 drops per 1 ounce of resin; and so 3% for the 2 ounces would be 2x15-30 drops.

For quantities of resin more than a few ounces it is more convenient to use a liquid measure to determine the amount of catalyst (hardener) to be added. A measuring beaker is the answer here, normally graduated in *millilitres*. The following measures then apply:

    5 millilitres equals 1% catalyst (hardener) per 1 pound of resin

    10 millilitres equals 2% catalyst (hardener) per 1 pound of resin

    15 millilitres equals 3% catalyst (hardener) per 1 pound of resin

    20 millilitres equals 4% catalyst (hardener) per 1 pound of resin

The same measures, of course, can apply if accelerator is to be added to the resin—or, in fact, any other additive. In the case of powdered accelerators or catalysts, measures should be done by weights, when table V can be used.

CHAPTER SIX

Other materials

Various other substances are used in the production of GRP mouldings, only some of which are essential. Others are used purely for improved appearance (e.g. colour), whilst fillers may be used to add 'body' to a moulding or casting, or to economise on resin. The only *essential* additional materials required, in fact, are polishes and release agents for preparing the surface of the mould, and suitable fluids for cleaning brushes and rollers. (Tools and equipment needed are described in Chapter 8).

Mould Polishes

About the best type of polish for a mould is a good *carnauba wax*. Most domestic and car-type hard wax polishes are based on carnauba wax, but may also contain other ingredients which can affect the setting of the gel coat, or even produce local adhesion. Silicone waxes must be avoided as these can have an inhibiting action on the gel coat resin. Also release agents will not dry over a silicone surface. In case of doubt, a wax polish should be tested for 'release' and 'adhesion' before being accepted as suitable.

Liquid and cream-type polishes are also available, specially formulated for GRP work. These produce a similar result to 'solid' wax polishes but are easier to apply. Final polishing is done when they have dried.

A good wax polish applied to a mould will also act as a release agent. However, as a general rule polishing should be followed with a coat of release agent.

Release Agents

The general type of release agent used is polyvinyl alcohol–known as PVA or PVAL. This is available as a concentrated solution for dilution with water or methylated spirits, or in ready-diluted strength (usually in meths). It may be coloured (typically green or blue) or clear. A coloured solution is preferred as it clearly indicates which areas of the mould surface have been covered when applied.

PVA is easy to apply since it can be sprayed, brushed or sponged on to the surface of the mould. One disadvantage, however, is that PVA has a low viscosity so its tends to drain off vertical surfaces, and can also accumulate in sharp corners where it will take a long time to dry. PVA can be used on its own over small, non-porous mould surfaces but on larger moulds it is more usual to use it as a second line of defence in conjunction with wax polishing.

PVA is also available in powder form, which can be dissolved in hot water to produce a suitable solution. The addition of a little glycerine is recommended to render the film slightly flexible, so that it can be stripped off the mould in a continuous sheet. The addition of alcohol to the solution, or the use of alcohol instead of water as a solvent, produces a solution which dries much more rapidly.

Cellulose acetate. Cellulose acetate dissolved in acetone, i.e.cellulose 'lacquer', is also an effective parting agent, particularly suitable for applying by spray. An additional coating of wax polish is, however, recommended for complete treatment. It should be noted that cellulose *nitrate* solutions are not suitable release agents, and many cellulose lacquers are based on nitrate rather than acetate.

Candle Wax. This is an effective parting agent, but rather difficult to apply evenly except to small moulds. In certain cases, however, it may be useful for treating undercuts.

Main properties of these types of release agents are summarised in table VI.

Sheet Release Agents

Where the mould lends itself to covering by draping with thin sheet material, the following can be used instead of applying parting agent direct to the surface of the mould.

Acetate sheet. Preferably in the form of cellophane (0.002-0.003 in thick) of the non-waterproofed kind (which contains lacquer and will not part from the mould). Note again that cellulose nitrate sheet ('celluloid') is not effective.

PVA sheet. Very effective, and available under the trade name of 'Pevalon'.

Polythene. Effective, but expensive and not readily available. It has the advantage of being a stretchable material.

The remaining materials described are those which may be incorporated in the GRP laminate itself.

Pigments

Pigments *can* be used for throughcolouring (i.e. mixed with the laminating resin), but are normally only used in the *gel coat.* A pigmented gel coat is the obvious and the most satisfactory method of producing a coloured moulding, although this will only produce a high class finish where the moulding is produced in a polished mould. It is almost impossible to produce a satisfactory self-coloured finish on the 'rough' side of a moulding where the surface has to be worked over to produce a good finish, particularly as a gloss colour will only show up the irregularity of the surface. For this reason the 'rough' sides of mouldings are best left uncoloured, or if colouring is thought necessary, sprayed with a matt finish (preferably with a flock or speckled effect).

It can be mentioned that despite the obvious advantages of a self-colour applied in the gel coat of a female moulding, some manufacturers of high class products still prefer to produce a 'plain' moulding and finish by spray painting. This is found in the car industry, for example, with some moulded GRP body shells.

As a general rule, no more pigment should be added than is necessary to achieve the required degree of colour or opacity as most pigments tend to detract from, rather than enhance, the mechanical properties of the resin. Some types of conventional pigments may also have an inhibiting action on the resin and must be avoided. These include black pigments based on carbon.

Pigments are normally produced in the form of solids which must be ground into a fine paste with a suitable vehicle—in this case the resin. Ready-prepared pigments can be obtained in the form of resin-pastes, and this is the best way of using them, although it is not always possible to know whether the paste is highly concentrated or dilute. A maximum of 5% pigment should not be exceeded, which in the case of a highly concentrated paste usually means a maximum of 10% paste. With a diluted pigment paste, a 10% addition to the resin may not give the required depth of colour or opacity.

A wide variety of colours is available as pigment pastes, covering virtually all requirements. Specific types may also be suitable for intermixing to obtain different shades. The fastness of the colour depends primarily on whether the particular pigment used is fugitive or not, and also whether the pigment contains a proportion of dye. In the latter case the colour may change during curing because of the oxidising action of the catalyst having a bleaching effect.

The addition of pigments may also affect the gel time of the resin. In some cases the gel time may be increased (commonly with blacks and blues); in others it may be shortened. This can only be found out by experience with particular pigments.

If pigments other than specified as suitable for polyester resins are to be used, then the effect of these on the resin (and possible change of colour with the resin) should be investigated first by a few simple trials. This could avoid disappointing results on a finished moulding. Such trials are unnecessary on polyester resin pigment pastes.

Translucent Colours

Compatible dyes are also available for colouring polyester resin. These are intended for use where translucent through-colouring is required, such as in the production of rooflight mouldings and imitation stained glass, etc. These are generally referred to as translucent colours. Unless specially formulated for use with polyester resin, their possible effect on gel time and curing should be investigated by trials first.

Translucent colours can best be produced by the addition of *translucent colour pastes* used in the proportion of 2% to 5% by weight of resin. Optimum proportion can only be determined by experiment, as this can vary with the colour selected. Too little translucent paste will result in a streaky appearance. Too much will reduce the translucency. It is usually better to err on the side of too much rather than too little.

Translucent colouring can be enhanced by backing a translucent coloured gel coat with a second gel coat pigment with opaque white, after allowing ample time for the first gel coat to harden (normally at least six hours).

Metallic Finishes

Metallic powders such as aluminium and bronze can be incorporated in the resin, but can be disappointing when used in the gel coat in a female mould. This is because a good metallic finish relies on the metallic particles aligning themselves in a preferred direction in a thin layer of 'carrier' medium. Metallic powders tend to become dispersed and random orientated in a thicker gel coat.

Quite outstanding effects can be produced by using brilliant aluminium, plastic or metallic coloured vinyl flakes 'puffed' on to the inside of the gel coat as it sets in the mould. A suitable technique has to be developed by trial and error, however. One method of dispensing flakes in this way is by squeezing them out from a punctured polybag.

The best results using coloured *metal flakes* to produce a metallic appearance are obtained only by *spraying* a mixture of resin and flakes. The same applies to the use of *polychromatic* pigments, which again can produce a 'metallic' finish. In both cases the proportion of resin to flakes (or pigment) should be about 1 part by weight to 8 parts resin.

Thixotropic Agents

Where non-sagging properties are required, thixotropic resins should be used (i.e. resins ready mixed with a thixotropic additive). Most gel coat resins are of thixotropic type. General purpose resins may or may not be thixotropic. A non-thixotropic resin can be converted into a thixotropic by the addition of a suitable agent such as hydrogenated castor oil or, more usually, silica aerogel and aerosil powder in proportions up to 5 per cent. A typical additive may consist of 4% aerogel and 1% aerosil powder. A problem with handling the latter is that it is very light and floats in the air, so is not only difficult to mix but can present a health hazard. If you do want to turn a non-thixotropic resin into a thixotropic resin it is best to use ready-compounded *thixotropic paste* for the additive.

Fillers

Fillers are inert substances, usually a powder, which may be added to liquid resin to give it more bulk and also 'through colour'. Because resin is relatively expensive, the use of fillers can reduce the cost of GRP moulding of a required thickness and at the same time somewhat increase its compressive strength. However, it is likely that the overall strength will be reduced if the proportion of fillers used is too generous. Also the introduction of fillers in the resin can make it more difficult to judge whether or not a lay-up is suitably consolidated with the exclusion of air bubbles, or introduce local weaknesses if the filler is not completely and uniformly mixed with the resin.

Fillers can be most useful where 'body' is required, or through-colouring is particularly desirable. Special types of fillers may also be used to improve both tensile

and impact strength. These would be fibrous type fillers, such as organic fibre, chopped glass fibre or macerated fabrics.

A further use of fillers is for rendering the resin in the form of paste rather than a liquid. In this form it can be used as a filler for car body repairs, etc., without the addition of further reinforcement. The usual combination is a pre-accelerated resin and separate powder comprising filler mixed with powdered catalyst. The two are mixed in suitable proportions to provide the necessary stiff paste for filling and stopping work, setting hard by cold-curing in the usual way. Alternatively, resin and filler may be mixed to provide one paste, catalyst being supplied as a separate paste. In this case both products can be tubed for convenience of use.

Simple resin fillers of this type may be based on rigid resins, setting as hard as a normal GRP moulding, or on flexible resins to give a slightly elastic solid when set. The latter have the advantage that they are easier to re-work for flatting down, etc. Other types of fillers may have reinforcement introduced, as well as filler, and may be suitable for the production of moulded shapes. Casting resins may also incorporate fillers, for reinforcement, colouring, or other decorative effects.

A basic requirement of any filler is that it should be inert and have no inhibiting effect on the resin cure. Also the filler material should not be subject to ageing or deterioration under the service conditions involved for the final product. The usual choice is a mineral filler, such as precipitated chalk, China clay, talc or whitening. These materials are satisfactory, provided they are pure and very finely powdered. They will mix uniformly with the resin, with the effect of increasing its viscosity, i.e. tending to make it become more paste-like. The higher the proportion of filler the stiffer the resin becomes

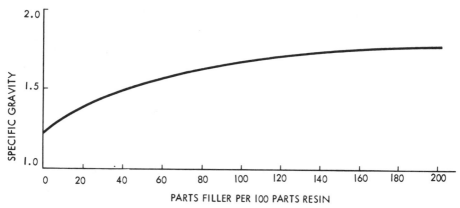

FIG. 6.1 INCREASE IN WEIGHT WITH FILLERS

for working. This effect is even more marked with the modern surface-treated calcium carbonate fillers, particularly crystalline types, which have become the preferred choice. These also improve the impact strength of the moulding, as well as producing a harder, more scratch-resistant surface. This type of filler is also used where moulding in light or bright colours is required, without going to the expense of titanium dioxide or other similar pigments possessing a high refractive index.

The use of fillers results in an increase in density of the resin, the specific gravity of the combination tending to approach that of the filler material with increasing proportion of fillers—see Fig. 6.1. At the same time the inherent shrinkage of the resin on setting is reduced—see Fig. 6.2. The latter can be a particularly favourable characteristic in the case of making castings.

The effect on impact strength is shown in Fig. 6.3, where the superior performance of a surface-treated filler is obvious.

On the other hand, the addition of filler tends to increase the gel time, which may

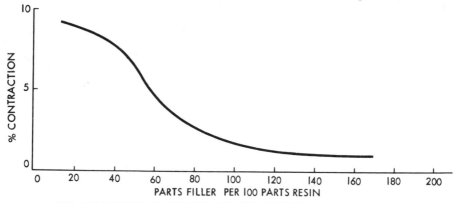

FIG. 6.2 SHRINKAGE RELATED TO PER CENT FILLER ADDED TO MIX

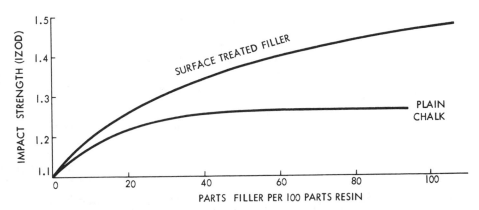

FIG. 6.3 IMPROVEMENT IN IMPACT STRENGTH WITH ADDITION OF FILLER

be a disadvantage, and, more important, an excess of fillers will tend to make the cured laminate brittle. For this reason, where fillers are used, it is generally recommended that the proportion of fillers to resin should not be in excess of 50:100. For general work, where fillers are used, the proportion is usually between 25 and 50 parts per 100 parts of resin, see table VII.

Use of other types of fillers can be summarised briefly:

Slate powder—for general 'bulking' of the resin, with the addition of a grey colour.

Mica powder—for casting and potting applications.

Silica flour—to improve abrasion resistance.

Iron powder—for moulding magnetic cores, etc.

Graphite—for moulding semi-conductors.

Asbestos powder—for self-extinguishing or flameproof mouldings.

Antimony oxide—for self-extinguishing mouldings.

Sawdust—for producing resin/filler mixes that set with the appearance of solid wood.

Vinyl flakes—for 'pearlescent' decorative effects.

Chalk and China clay are also used in very high proportions for making cold-setting 'china castings'. In this case only enough resin is used to provide a suitable bond for the powder. Similarly, metal powder fillers are used for producing 'cold casting' metals on the same basis.

See also Chapter 7 for working out quantities of materials required.

Sand and Grit

For producing a non-slip or hard wearing surface on a GRP moulding sand or carborundum grit can be used as a 'surface filler' on the initial gel coat or over a final surface coating of resin, sprinkled in place before the resin has set. Sand will produce a natural light colour non-slip surface. Carborundum grit will produce a dark surface with very hard wearing properties (i.e. much more resistant to abrasion than a normal gel coat finish).

Acetone

Acetone is a solvent for polyester resins, but only in their uncured state. Its particular use is for cleaning resin off brushes,

TABLE VI   RELEASE AGENTS

Type	Method of Application	Suitable types of moulds	Removal	Remarks
Hard Wax (Wax Polishes)	Apply generously then polish	GRP, plastic, hardboard, wood, etc.	Xylene, or scrub with strong detergent	Silicone-waxes should be avoided. Additional protection given by further coat of PVA
Wax Emulsions	Smear on, leave to dry, then polish	Plaster, GRP, plastic hardboard, wood, etc.	Xylene or scrub with strong detergent	Suitable for one-coat treatment on all kinds of moulds
Candle Wax	Smear on	Small moulds and undercuts	Warm to melt	Difficulty to apply evenly
PVA	Spray, brush or sponge (latter often easiest)	GRP, and all moulds with hard, sealed surface	Wash with warm water, or strip off if possible	
Cellulose Acetate	Spray preferred	GRP, plastic, hardboard, wood, etc.	Cellulose thinners	Final wax polishing recommended

rollers, etc. *before* the resin has set hard. Another use of acetone is for the treatment of specimens prior to embedding in cast resin—see chapter 13 on Casting, Potting and Encapsulation.

Some words of caution. Pure acetone is the material to use. 'Commercial' acetone is a reclaimed product which may contain potentially dangerous chemicals, particularly caustic soda, which can be harmful to hands, etc. Sensitive skins will also be harmed by pure acetone.

Acetone has only a mild attack on *cured* polyester resins.

Cellulose Thinners

Cellulose thinners can also be used for cleaning brushes, rollers, etc., provided the resin has not set hard. It is less expensive than acetone, but not as effective in this respect. Again it can attack sensitive skins.

Styrene

Styrene is available as a separate liquid for thinning resins, but its use for this purpose should be restricted to a very limited number of applications. It can, for example, prove useful for thinning resins to be

TABLE VII   WEIGHT OF FILLERS REQUIRED
(Note: Usual proportions recommended are 25–50%)
(Weight in pounds, except where noted)

Weight of Resin	Per cent Filler						
	20	25	50	75	100	125	150
10 lb	2.0	2.5	5.0	7.5	10	12.5	15
5 lb	1.0	1.25	2.5	3.75	5	6.25	7.5
2 lb	6.4 oz	8 oz	1.0	1.5	2	2.5	3
1 lb	3.2 oz	4 oz	8 oz	12 oz	1	1.25	1.5
8 oz	1.6 oz	2 oz	4 oz	6 oz	10 oz	10 oz	12 oz
4 oz	0.8 oz	1 oz	2 oz	3 oz	4 oz	5 oz	6 oz
2 oz	0.4 oz	$\frac{1}{2}$ oz	1 oz	$1\frac{1}{2}$ oz	2 oz	$2\frac{1}{2}$ oz	3 oz

painted on wood as a *primer* coat (i.e. for sealing purposes). In this case the amount of styrene used should not be more than 1 part styrene to 20 parts resin. It should never normally be used for thinning a resin to make it sprayable—a resin with the right viscosity *for* spraying should be used. If it *is* strictly necessary to thin a resin to make it spray better, then not more than 1 part styrene per 30 parts of resin should be used. Thinning an over-aged resin which has become semi-hardened with styrene will not make the resin usable.

Resin Stripper

Various caustic solutions are available as brush cleaning solutions and, in more concentrated form, as *resin stripper.* Resin stripper will dissolve solidified resin and so can be used to renovate brushes which have become hardened and also remove cured resin adhering to tools, etc. Several hours soaking (e.g. overnight) is necessary to clean brushes in this way, which then need to be washed out *thoroughly* in water and dried.

Resin stripper is a poisonous substance, giving off toxic fumes which should not be breathed. It can also produce burns in contact with skin—wash off *immediately* in running water if it is splashed onto your hands or face.

CHAPTER SEVEN

Quantities required

The following materials will be required for producing laminates in a mould, or making moulds themselves from a model or plug. Quantities of each required are then based on the surface area involved.

(i) Polish for mould (or plug).
(ii) Release agent for mould.
(iii) Gel coat resin.
(iv) Surface tissue layer.
(v) Chopped strand mat (or other reinforcement material).
(vi) Final layer of surface tissue, if to be used.
(vii) Final (inside) gel coat, if to be used.
(viii) Lay-up resin.

Note: in many cases (vi) and (vii) are omitted. In other cases additional glass and resin may be needed for glassing over ribs, reinforcements, etc. and doubling up certain areas for additional strength.

(i) Polish

Quantities for polish are difficult to estimate for individual jobs. Polish is usually bought as a stock material to cover a number of jobs.

(ii) Release Agent

PVA release agent is commonly sold in its ready-to-use diluted form by *pounds* weight or by *volume* in litres (e.g. a standard polybottle holds 5 litres or approximately 11 lb). The amount used to produce an overall coating of the mould surface will depend on whether it is applied by *spray* or brush.

For *spray* application of release agent, estimate quantities required for an individual job on the basis:—

1 *pound* of release agent or $\frac{1}{2}$ *litre* of release agent will cover 25 sq. ft. ($2\frac{1}{3}$ sq. metres) with two mist coats.

For *brush* application of release agent, estimate quantity required on the basis:

1 *pound* of release agent or $\frac{1}{2}$ *litre* will cover 15 sq. ft. ($1\frac{1}{2}$ sq. metres).

(iii) Gel Coat Resin

Quantity required can be estimated quite accurately on the basis of 2 ounce (weight) of resin per square foot of mould area, or $10\frac{3}{4}$ ounces per sq. metre; or 300 grammes per sq. metre.

(iv) Surface Tissue Layer

Quantity required is equal to the surface area of the mould plus, say 10% to allow for wastage. If step (vi) is included in the specification, double this amount.

Surface tissue is normally sold in rolls of various widths (usually 12 in) containing so many square metres. Alternatively, smaller quantities will be priced per square metre. If the surface area calculation is in square feet, divide by 10 to give area in square metres.

(v) Chopped Strand Mat

Chopped strand mat is normally sold by *weight*. The quantity required is governed by surface area involved and the *thickness* of laminate required. When working out the surface area, allow an extra 5% to be on the safe side and allow for edge trimming—i.e. 10% extra overall. The thickness is rendered in terms of equivalent *total glass weight* for estimating purposes.

It does not matter how this thickness is worked out. You can work on so many layers of a single (or mixed) weight(s) of CSM to arrive at a final thickness *dimension* or take a total glass weight required (e.g. a recommended figure) and from this decide the number of layers of a particular *weight* of CSM (or particular mixture of weights).

The simplest way is to work with the *same* weight of CSM in each layer, then the *amount* of that weight of CSM required is the total glass weight. If you want to mix layers of different thicknesses, then you will have to calculate total glass weights for *each* individual thickness.

The following table is designed to show quantities required working either with actual thickness required, or total glass weight.

(vi) Glass Cloth

Woven glass fabrics are produced in continuous rolls in a standard width of nominally 36in (91cm), although other widths may sometimes be available. They are normally sold cut to length required and priced per square metre. 'Thickness' is specified by weight, the usual weights being 110g/m², 175g/m² and 330g/m² for scrim (open weave fabric); and from 280g/m² upwards for other woven fab-

TABLE VIII   AMOUNT OF CHOPPED STRAND MAT REQUIRED

Thickness of laminate required nominal dimension		glass weight		Amount of chopped strand mat required per 10ft² _or_ per metre²	
in	mm	oz/ft²	g/m²	lb	kg
$\frac{1}{32}$	0.8	1	300	0.7	0.3
$\frac{3}{64}$	1.2	$1\frac{1}{2}$	450	1.0	0.5
$\frac{1}{16}$	1.5	2	600	1.4	0.65
$\frac{3}{32}$	2.4	3	900	2.1	1.0
$\frac{1}{8}$	3	$3\frac{1}{2}$	1050	2.4	1.15
$\frac{9}{64}$	3.5	4	1200	2.8	1.3
$\frac{5}{32}$	4	$4\frac{1}{2}$	1350	3.1	1.4
$\frac{3}{16}$	5	6	1800	4.2	2.0
$\frac{15}{64}$	6	$7\frac{1}{2}$	2250	5.2	2.4
$\frac{1}{4}$	6.5	8	2400	5.6	2.6
$\frac{9}{32}$	7	9	2700	6.3	2.9
$\frac{5}{16}$	8	10	3000	7.0	3.2
$\frac{11}{32}$	9	$11\frac{1}{2}$	3450	7.3	3.33
$\frac{3}{8}$	10	12	3600	8.4	3.8
$\frac{29}{64}$	11.5	$14\frac{1}{2}$	4350	10.2	4.6
$\frac{1}{2}$	12.5	16	4800	11.2	5.0

Specified weight g/m²	Approx. equivalent weight ounces/sq. yard	ounces/sq. feet
110	3.3	$\frac{1}{3}$
175	5¼	$\frac{1}{2}$
280	8	1
300	9	1
450	13½	1½
560	16	1¾
600	18	2
830	24	2½

rics. The above equivalent values will be a useful guide in deciding the weight required.

(vii) Glassfibre Tape

Glassfibre tapes are produced in a wide range of widths from ¼in (6.5mm) up to 6in (150mm). Sizes smaller than 1in (25mm) width may be more difficult to locate. Glassfibre tape is sold by the metre length, or in rolls (usually 50 metres).

(viii) Lay-up Resin

Resin is sold by weight. The amount of resin required is equal to the total glass weight multiplied by the intended (or anticipated) resin to glass ratio. The following table is worked out for rapid solutions to resin requirements for chopped strand mat mouldings.

Note: lay-up resins normally include accelerator. Price of resin also normally

TABLE IX   WEIGHT OF RESIN REQUIRED WITH CSM

| Total glass weight | | Weight of resin per 10 sq. ft. *or* per sq. metre Resin to glass ratio | | | | | | | | | |
| oz/ft² | g/m² | 3.5 | | 3 | | 2.75 | 2.5 | | 2.25 | 2.0 | |
		lb	kg	lb	kg	lb	lb	kg	lb	lb	kg
1	300	2¼	1.0	1⅞	0.85	1¾	1⅝	0.71	1¼	1¼	0.57
1½	450	3¼	1.5	2¾	1.30	2½	2½	1.07	2	1⅞	0.85
2	600	4½	2.0	3¾	1.70	3½	3⅛	1.93	3	2½	1.14
3	900	6½	3.0	5⅝	2.60	5¼	4¾	2.14	4¼	3¾	1.70
3½	1050	7⅝	3.5	6½	3.00	6	5½	2.50	5	4⅜	2.00
4	1200	8¾	4.0	7½	3.40	6⅞	6¼	2.86	5⅝	5	2.27
4½	1350	10	4.5	8½	3.85	7¾	7	3.21	6⅜	5⅝	2.55
6	1800	13⅛	6	11¼	5.19	10½	9⅜	4.28	8½	7.9	3.40
7½	2250	16½	7.5	14	6.43	13	11¾	5.36	10½	9⅜	4.25
8	2400	17½	8	15	6.80	13¾	12½	5.71	11¼	10	4.54
9	2700	20	9	17	7.71	15½	14	6.43	12⅝	11¼	5.10
10	3000	22	10	18¾	8.57	17¼	15⅝	7.14	14	12½	5.68
11½	3450	25	11.5	21½	9.85	20	18	8.21	16¼	14⅜	6.52
12	3600	26¼	12	22½	10.30	20½	18¾	8.57	16⅞	15	6.80
14½	4350	32	14.5	27	12.50	25	22⅝	10.35	20½	18⅛	8.23
16	4800	35	16.0	30	13.60	27½	25	11.43	22½	20	9.08

includes matching quantity of catalyst.

In the case of woven glass fabric reinforcement or rovings, amount of resin required can be taken as the same as the weight of glass. Normally cloth or rovings will only be used in part of the laminate, so adjust resin quantities required accordingly.

Where a final layer of surfacing tissue (vi) and/or a final 'inside' gel coat is to be applied (viii), allow for extra resin on the basis of 2 ounces/sq. ft (300 grammes per square metre).

Other Materials

Other materials which might be included, e.g. colour pastes and/or fillers are normally based on a specific proportion of the resin weight to which they are added. Quantities required can thus be calculated directly from the resin weight involved and previously determined, e.g.:—

Colour pastes—amount required is 10% of the weight of gel coat resin estimated for. Colour pastes are normally only used in the gel coat, and 10% represents a *maximum* recommended proportion. You may need to use less.

Fillers—if used are normally only added to the laminating (or casting) resin in recommended proportions up to a maximum of about 40% by weight. Amount of filler required is therefore X% of the laminating resin weight, where X is the recommended proportion for use.

Tools and equipment

Glass fibre is not exactly the easiest material to work with. Chopped strand mat is difficult to cut neatly to the shapes required and if over-handled pulls apart. Woven glass cloth and rovings can be difficult to cut at all. And once wetted with resin becomes a sticky, messy material which sometimes defies manipulation into the area required. Nevertheless the finished product—a fully cured moulding—should be reward enough for efforts properly applied.

Accepting that laying up a glass fibre moulding will be messy work, wear old clothes, or a suitable protective overall or apron, and protect the working area from surplus resin which can stick and harden on it, and be very difficult to remove. Hands can be protected by using a barrier cream or by wearing thin rubber gloves (disposable polythene gloves are particularly recommended as being cheap and easy to work in).

As far as possible, prepare everything needed before you start spreading resin. Cut all the necessary surface tissue and mat or cloth to length or shape in 'clean' conditions. A reasonably large pair of scissors can be used for cutting glass reinforcement, or a *really* sharp knife can be easiest to use on surfacing tissue or woven cloth. The knife will soon be blunted, so a preferred type here is one with a replaceable blade.

Some form of weighing machine is needed to measure out the required quantities of resin, together with suitable measures for arriving at the correct proportion of catalyst to be used. Alternatively, liquid measures can be used throughout.

Other tools and equipment required are concerned with the application of resin and laying up the laminate and finally for cutting and trimming the edges of the hardened moulding to final shape.

Spraying is undoubtedly the best method of *applying* resin where it is needed, and particularly for the application of the gel coat to the inside of the mould. However, to be properly effective a spray gun capable of spraying the correct proportions of resin and hardener simultaneously is needed. The cost of such equipment is normally outside the budget of the amateur, and certainly not justified for occasional projects. Even a large proportion of professional products do not use spray application, except for the gel coat. Brushwork is thus a broad standard for resin application.

Spraying the *release agent* onto the mould is, however, a possibility for most amateurs. Only a simple low pressure sprayer is needed, for the liquid used is very thin and does not have to be mixed with anything.

Brushes for Gel Coats

For local application of *gel coats,* flat brushes with soft bristles are needed. The size depends on the area worked. For large

STIFF BRISTLE BRUSHES
(PREFERABLE ROUND SECTION)
FOR DABBING AND WETTING
OUT REINFORCEMENT

FLAT BRUSHES WITH
SOFT BRISTLES FOR
GEL COAT APPLICATION

CUT SHORT TO
IMPROVE STIPPLING ACTION

FIG. 8.1 BRUSHES FOR GRP HAND LAY-UP

areas use a 2 in or 3 in brush; although 1 in or even $\frac{3}{4}$ in brushes will be more suitable for general work.

Ordinary soft paintbrushes are suitable for gel coat application, although the preference is for ones with white or colourless bristles rather than black bristles, so that loose bristles will not show up.

Lambswool paint rollers can also be used for applying the gel coat on large flat areas, but although this speeds the work the resulting thickness of resin is usually inadequate from a single coating. The job, therefore, has to be done at least twice, allowing each coat to gel before applying the next.

Brushes for Laminating Resins

You can use the same brush(es) for applying laminating resins, but rather larger, stiffer brushes are preferred. The best type is a stiff circular brush—even cutting down the length of bristles if necessary to give extra stiffness—Fig. 8.1. The reason for using a stiff brush is that unlike gel coats which are *painted* on to the mould surfaces, laminating resin has to be worked into the glass fibre layer(s). If you try to *paint* resin on to chopped strand mat you will only end up by pulling the mat all over the place. Resin has to be applied with a

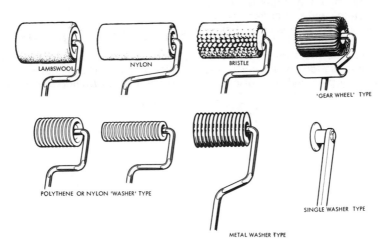

LAMBSWOOL

NYLON

BRISTLE

'GEAR WHEEL' TYPE

POLYTHENE OR NYLON 'WASHER' TYPE

SINGLE WASHER TYPE

METAL WASHER TYPE

FIG. 8.2 ROLLERS FOR GRP HAND LAY-UP

49

'stippling' or *dabbing* action to keep the mat in place and at the same time wet it out uniformly with resin.

Rollers (Fig. 8.2)

Rollers should then be used for *consolidating* each layer of laminate in turn. This *can* also be done with a brush, but you will use much more resin and not achieve the same degree of consolidation, usually resulting in an uneven thickness and a high possibility of trapped air pockets. There is no substitute for a roller for consolidating the laminate layers in hand lay-up, particularly where large areas are involved. A roller produces a more uniform 'squeegeeing' effect, and the job can be done much faster.

Ordinary paint rollers are useless for such a job. There are several special types of rollers produced for GRP laminating work, but the two best are the split *metal washer type* and the *paddle wheel* type.

A *metal washer* roller consists of a series of washers separated by smaller diameter size washers mounted together on a spindle and frame with a wooden handle. Typical sizes are $\frac{3}{4}$ in diameter by 3 in height and $1\frac{1}{2}$ in diameter by 6 in or 3 in height, or even smaller. It is the strongest type of roller, and thus the longest lasting and is the type usually preferred. It is also pro-

duced in plastic counterpart with nylon or polythene washers instead of metal. Both these types are easier to clean, but are not as durable. There are also single wheel metal and plastic rollers for getting into awkward corners.

A *paddle wheel* roller is basically a length of aluminium tube cast with lengthways ridges (i.e. the 'gaps' in the roller surface are lengthwise rather than diameter-wise as on the metal washer roller). In use, it is equally effective in squeezing out trapped air bubbles. Sizes available are similar to metal washer rollers.

'Soft' rollers may be better to use on certain jobs—e.g. a plastic roller or a *bristle* roller. Note, too, that several sizes of rollers may be useful—long rollers for working over large surfaces and short rollers for working in restricted corners, etc. Alternatively, a stiff brush can be used in such places.

Rollers can be cleaned in the same solution as brushes, although metal rollers are often more conveniently cleaned by burning off the resin and then scraping clean.

Knives (see Fig. 8.3)

Palette knives are useful for working pigments and fillers into the resin, and for small stopping or filling jobs using resin-

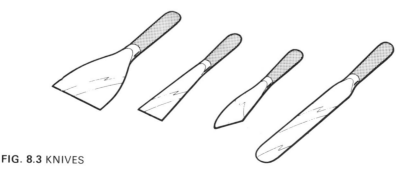

FIG. 8.3 KNIVES

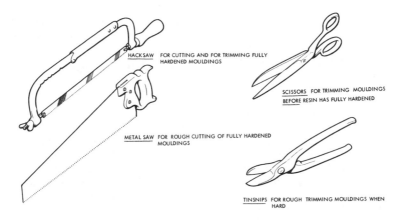

FIG. 8.4 CUTTING AND TRIMMING TOOLS

filler. Larger jobs of this nature can be tackled best with conventional putty knives.

Cutting Tools (see Fig. 8.4)

Once hardened off, a GRP moulding will be too hard to be cut or trimmed with woodworking tools, and getting a clean cut edge on the moulding can be hard work. Either a metal-cutting saw or a hacksaw must be used. The latter makes the neatest job, using a blade with 32 teeth to the inch. The blade should be discarded as soon as it shows signs of becoming blunted.

Note here that much effort can often be saved by trimming the edge of a moulding during the hardening time, i.e. before the GRP has reached its full hardened strength. At this stage trimming can still be done with a sharp knife, or possibly even scissors. At a slightly later stage, but before the GRP has set really hard, trimming can be done with tinsnips.

Sanding Discs

These should be of 'hard' type with a coarse grit on a tough backing. Fine abrasive discs will clog too rapidly to be effective. Sanding discs used on power drills are the quickest and easiest way of final-trimming edges, or removing rough spots or irregularities on the surface of finished laminates.

A sanding disc, or orbital sander, is also effective for flatting down resin-filler when set. If the build-up is excessive, a 'Surform' tool with a new blade should be used first to level off as far as possible. This will be quicker than using a sanding disc, and will also greatly increase the life of the disc. A 'Surform' tool is also useful for rough shaping and trimming all GRP mouldings.

Files

To cut effectively, files should be of coarse metal-cutting type, and new. The life of a file used on glass fibre is very limited, and it should be discarded when it shows signs of becoming blunt.

Drills

Glass fibre must be considered as metal for the purpose of drilling. Only high speed steel twist drills should be used, with the lowest possible drilling speed (particularly with larger drill sizes). Drilling should always be done from the gel coat side, and the other side of the moulding backed up with a block of wood to limit the extent of tearing or cracking when the drill breaks through. A hole drilled from the opposite side will almost invariably damage the gel coat, even if backed up.

Drills used for drilling glass fibre should always be sharp, and ground to the same point angle as for cutting metals. In the case of drill sizes of $\frac{3}{8}$in and above, the point angle of the drill can be reduced with some advantage. No lubricant is normally required, but if a drill does show signs of running hot, water can be used to cool it.

Abrasive Papers

Any 'finish sanding' on GRP mouldings should always be done with wet and dry abrasive papers, used wet and frequently rinsed off to clean. Some authorities also recommend the addition of a little soap to the rinsing water to act as a lubricant.

For 'rough' sanding 240 grit will be suitable. Progressively finer grades down to 500 or even 600 grit can be used for final smoothing. The surface can be further improved by buffing and polishing with metal polish, polishing compound or jeweller's rouge. A final overall finish can be given by wax polishing, provided this is acceptable to the application.

CHAPTER NINE

Design in GRP

The general properties which make GRP an attractive structural material are:

(i) High strength with low weight.

(ii) High impact strength combined with great resilience.

(iii) Suitability for making products of any size.

(iv) Resistance to weather, chemicals, water, most oils, spirits, acids, alkalis and solvents.

(v) Dimensionally stable — retains shape under mechanical stress and temperature extremes–from below freezing point to above 250°f (120°C), i.e. well above the boiling point of water.

(vi) Non-conductive, with good electrical properties, and ability to pass radio waves.

(vii) Low thermal conductivity; transmitting less than half the heat of glass.

(viii) Naturally translucent and may be coloured as desired.

(ix) Negligible water absorption with retention of shape and strength when constantly immersed.

(x) Easy to produce GRP mouldings without expensive equipment.

In the main design in GRP for stressing purposes is done on empirical lines. That virtually means 'guesstimating' the thicknesses required, and whether or not additional local reinforcement or stiffening may be required.

This, together with working to recommended figures for glass weight for particular applications, is the usual method adopted in the design of GRP components. For the technically minded, however, it is readily possible to calculate the various properties of a prepared laminate–e.g. its strength in tension, compression, bending (and the amount of deflection under bending loads), shear, etc.–see under the appropriate headings in the Appendix section. At the same time, however, mechanical properties of GRP laminates are likely to be variable with lay-up technique employed, as well as the type of reinforcement used. Thus the specific figures for physical properties given in the Appendix are not necessarily applicable directly to all GRP mouldings using the same reinforcement.

Deflection under Bending Loads

Almost without exception, GRP mouldings are relatively thin and thus when stressed in compression will tend to fail by bending long before the material is stressed to anywhere near its compressive limit. Under such conditions the material is put into shear.

The main call when designing GRP mouldings for withstanding compressive loads, therefore, is to provide adequate stiffness to resist buckling and delay the point of ultimate failure which would

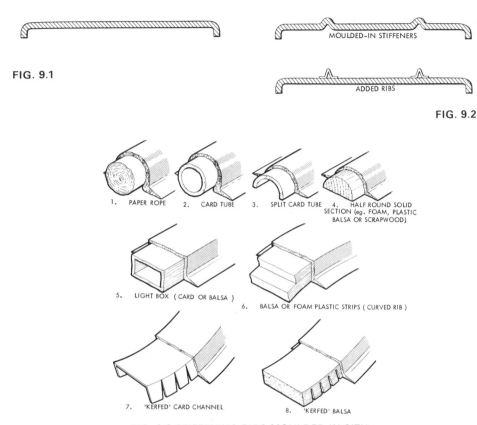

FIG. 9.1

MOULDED-IN STIFFENERS

ADDED RIBS

FIG. 9.2

1. PAPER ROPE   2. CARD TUBE   3. SPLIT CARD TUBE   4. HALF ROUND SOLID SECTION (eg. FOAM, PLASTIC BALSA OR SCRAPWOOD)

5. LIGHT BOX (CARD OR BALSA)

6. BALSA OR FOAM PLASTIC STRIPS (CURVED RIB)

7. 'KERFED' CARD CHANNEL

8. 'KERFED' BALSA

FIG. 9.3 STIFFENING RIBS MOULDED IN SITU

otherwise result from the high shear stresses, developed through buckling.

Exactly similar requirements usually apply where the GRP moulding is subject to bending loads. Because of the relatively low elastic modulus, GRP mouldings tend to have large deflections under bending loads. Apart from the fact that this will also produce high shear forces, large deflections are usually undesirable. Again, therefore, the primary requirement is usually for extra stiffening or rigidity to be built into the design.

Flat panels can be stiffened by introducing flanged edges—Fig. 9.1. This has the effect of providing a supported rather than a free edge. Further stiffening can then be introduced by adding moulded-in corrugations running in an appropriate direction, or directions, in the panel itself. Alternatively, separate stiffeners can be added to the panel after moulding. Either method can provide entirely satisfactory results see Fig. 9.2.

Some forms of separate stiffeners are shown in Fig. 9.3. Essentially these are

RIB APPLIED TOO SOON AFTER MOULDING

SHRINKAGE

FIG. 9.4

'girder' sections formed in glass mat. A suitable core material is only needed to enable such sections to be moulded on to the main moulding, with additional mat, and do not, or need not, contribute to the actual stiffening strength. Thus inexpensive lightweight materials may be

ment in the regions where more stiffness is required. The two methods may be used together, and also in conjunction with moulded-in or added on stiffeners.

Where additional layers of reinforcement are used to increase local stiffness or strength, the increase in cross section

'FORM' STIFFNESS

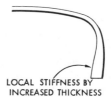

LOCAL STIFFNESS BY INCREASED THICKNESS   **FIG. 9.5**

used for stiffener cores or forms. This is a simpler method of adding separate stiffeners by moulding the GRP sections separately and then attaching them as finished mouldings.

An important point when adding stiffening ribs to a GRP moulding is that the moulding should be set hard before the additional ribs are added. If added on too soon, shrinkage can produce a distortion of the original moulding—see Fig. 9.4.

Stiffness can also be produced in other ways. The form of the moulding itself can provide inherent stiffness. Thus dished or curved cross-sections will be inherently stiffer than flat panels (9.5). A further method of increasing stiffness locally is by building up additional layers of reinforce-

produced should be progressive. Thus a concentrated build-up is bad, as it introduces a stress raiser or potential weakness at the point of abrupt change of cross-section (Fig. 9.6). The additional thickness should be built up progressively, so that the change of section is gradual and reasonably uniform.

Complete GRP mouldings of large size are, of course, also commonly stiffened with internal ribs, frames or added members, often of wood, which are glassed in place in the finished moulding (Fig. 9.7). This is particularly applicable in the case of boat hull mouldings. Lugs, brackets and other sections may also be required, either glassed in, or bolted, screwed or riveted in place. The choice between bonding or

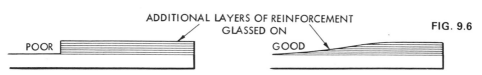

ADDITIONAL LAYERS OF REINFORCEMENT GLASSED ON

FIG. 9.6

POOR

GOOD

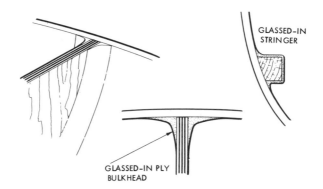

GLASSED-IN
STRINGER

GLASSED-IN PLY
BULKHEAD

FIG. 9.7

mechanical fastening in such cases will depend largely on the nature of the fitting involved, its function, and the material from which it is made. Reinforcements to the moulding itself are invariably bonded in, to give maximum strength. Additional fittings are preferably bonded in, but may need further treatment.

mencement of the hardening process at normal room temperatures is recommended for a complete adhesion. Too much reliance should not be placed on the resin for filling gaps, as it is naturally hard and brittle, and without glass reinforcing is liable to fracture.

Edge-to-edge joining of polyester

FIG. 9.8

The successful use of polyester resin as an adhesive depends to a great extent on the nature of the surfaces to be joined, as well as the type of joint made. Polyester to polyester joints should have an ample overlap where practical, and to ensure a first class bond, should be made before the resin has fully cured out in the parts to be joined. Up to six hours after the com-

sheets is not to be recommended, but if it is unavoidable, a good lap at the 'back' of the laminate, formed of several layers of cloth or tape, can be used (Fig. 9.8). Joining other materials to polyester by means of the resin largely depends on the nature of the material. As the field of possible materials is so wide, the best approach is to try out a specimen piece and so discover

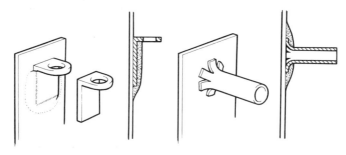

FIG. 9.9

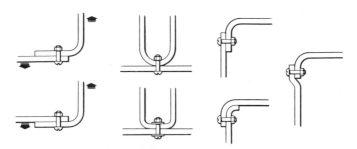

FIG. 9.10

whether the method would be satisfactory. Generally speaking any materials that have absorbent surfaces are no problem; hard polished surfaces such as on glass, some plastics, and polished metal are not practical to stick with the resin, as under stress it will break away cleanly. The resin will adhere well to a roughened metal surface, as the surface gives a sufficient 'key' for the resin to stick. Small metal brackets for joining other parts to a laminate are best moulded into the job as it is laid up. The brackets should have a sufficient flat area in contact with the resin, and should have several layers of cloth or mat, cut with a good overlap, laid over the bracket—see Fig. 9.9. Brackets moulded-in, in this manner, will be amply strong and the thickening of the laminate locally will help to distribute the load.

Screws, rivets and bolts are used for joining laminates, with and without the addition of resin. The main consideration is to avoid putting too great a stress on the local area at the attachment joint. Washers under the heads help to spread the load, and reference to table X giving minimum edge distance, hole sizes and thicknesses for countersinking, and to Fig. 9.10, will give some idea of the requirements in this direction.

When designing a moulding it is essential to think of the material as one of variable thickness and to determine the *amount of glass reinforcement* required in each part, or at specific points, bearing in mind the shape and rigidity required. In fact, if the moulding is rigid enough the other factors, such as tensile and compressive strength, resistance to shear, etc., are amply covered. It is easy to vary the thickness of the laminate at any point by adding extra layers of glass fibre. Obviously the best, lightest and most

TABLE X   EDGE DISTANCES AND LAMINATE THICKNESS

Rivet diameter		Laminate thickness	Edge distance (minimum)	Minimum laminate thickness for countersinking
$\frac{3}{32}$		$\frac{1}{8}$	$\frac{5}{16}$	.080
$\frac{1}{8}$		$\frac{3}{16}$	$\frac{3}{8}$	.090
$\frac{5}{32}$		$\frac{1}{4}$	$\frac{1}{2}$	.100
$\frac{3}{16}$	over	$\frac{1}{4}$	$\frac{1}{2}$	.110

All measurements in inches

economic moulding can be produced in this way.

It is far better to specify the *amount* of glass fibre in any part of a moulding than to specify the *thickness* as, by varying the ratio of glass to resin, laminates of the same thickness can have vastly different strengths. By specifying the amount of glass, laminates of different thickness due to varying amounts of resin will then have similar strength figures.

For further information on Design in GRP, see: Chapter 20 SANDWICH CONSTRUCTION.

Appendix 1—for details of laminate thicknesses.

Appendix 2—for details of strength of laminates.

Appendix 3—for details of weights of laminates.

Appendix 9—for working out deflections and stresses in sandwich beams.

CHAPTER TEN

Making moulds

A mould which duplicates the shape of the finished article is an *essential* feature for producing a GRP laminate. There are two basic types of mould—a *male* mould which is an exact pattern *over* which the laminate is formed, and a *female* mould which is a recessed shape duplicating the pattern *into* which the laminate is formed—Fig. 10.1.

Choice of the type of mould depends on which is to be the smooth side of the finishing moulding, this always being the side laid up in contact with the mould. Thus shapes like car body panels, boat hulls, and so on would normally be laid up in *female* moulds to produce a smooth surface on the outer side. Shapes like baths, basins, etc., would be laid up on a *male* mould, so that again the side that shows on the finished job is smooth. In other cases it may not matter which side of the laminate is smooth, when the choice of mould type can be based on which is the simplest to make, or which would be the

best side for the smooth surface judged from a functional rather than a decorative point of view.

Note here that a female mould produces a *male moulding* characterised by a smooth outer surface, whereas a male mould produces a *female moulding* with a smooth inner surface. It follows that a female *moulding* produced on a male mould can also make a female *mould* and vice versa.

Materials for Making Moulds

Moulds can be constructed from almost any material—plasticine, clay, plaster, wood, hardboard, ply, sheet metal. However, best results with female moulds are undoubtedly obtained by making the mould itself in GRP, which means a two-stage process of construction.

If the appearance given by a male mould is acceptable, this can result in consider-

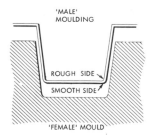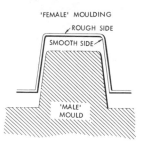

FIG. 10.1 THE TWO BASIC TYPES OF MOULDS

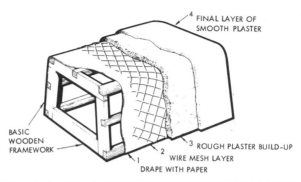

FIG. 10.2 SIMPLE PLASTER PATTERN CONSTRUCTION FOR LARGE SHAPES

able savings in time, materials and expense. All you need is a full size (three dimensional) pattern which can be used as the mould, the only necessity being to give it a smooth, non-absorbent finish.

The same technique can be applied to a female mould, but unless restricted to simple shapes and forms, the making and finishing of the pattern can become quite difficult. Remember that any pattern made for direct use as a mould must be a reverse image of the final shape required. Cost may be the deciding factor. For small objects the making of a female mould in GRP for one-off jobs is usually more than justified, because of the simple plug construction that can be used. With a large object, the more difficult job of making a reverse image pattern to act as a female mould can be worthwhile, because of the considerable saving in glass fibre and resin otherwise involved in making a GRP mould.

Do not overlook the possibilities of using an existing article as a pattern for a

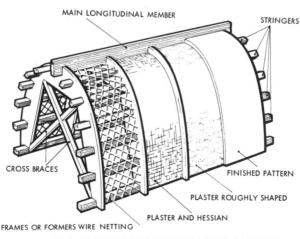

FIG. 10.3 MORE ELABORATE PLASTER PATTERN

mould, or as a basic shape which can be built upon to produce a pattern or plug. This can often save considerable time and effort in pattern making.

The Pattern or 'Plug'

Full size patterns, whether for use as plugs or direct moulds, have one thing in common—they must be finished to a perfectly smooth surface. Also, of course, they must duplicate the shape required faithfully. The materials used can be selected on the basis of providing the simplest, cheapest and quickest method of construction. In some cases an .existing object can be used directly as a plug, provided it is of suitable shape and the surface is, or can be, finished glass smooth.

Use of Wood

Wood is an obvious choice for making small patterns or plugs, balsa wood being particularly recommended because of the ease with which blocks and sheet can be cemented together to produce a basic form and the ease with which balsa can be carved to shape. The main difficulty with this material is the considerable time and effort needed to seal the grain and obtain a final glass-smooth surface. The cost of balsa also excludes its use for larger jobs.

Plaster Patterns

For large jobs, plaster can be the cheapest and simplest answer for large shapes, unless the form required can be built up simply from sheet hardboard. A plaster pattern can be built up around a rough mock-up of the shape, to save time, weight and the amount of plaster used. An example of a simple mock-up is shown in Fig. 10.2. This is then draped with brown paper, followed by a layer of wire mesh on which the plaster is trowelled and built up to a suitable thickness. The wire mesh provides a base on which to lay the plaster and the paper backing prevents it falling through whilst still wet. On larger patterns it may be necessary to support the plaster by draping the wire mesh with a further layer of hessian, or hessian soaked in plaster. In this case a wider mesh can be used see Fig. 10.3.

The final coat of plaster should be trowelled on and smoothed out as far as possible. When set, it must be worked over to produce a uniform, smooth surface. The surface will be quite porous, so will require sealing before it can be used as a plug (or a mould). Cellulose fillers are particularly recommended for sealing plaster for they provide a good surface which can be further rubbed down with fine wet or dry abrasive. Alternatively, several coats of shellac or two or three coats of any two-part synthetic resin sealer or varnish can be used.

Composite Constructions

Composite construction is also a possibility. A basic shape may be built up in 'box' form from hardboard, and the shape further extended by plasticine or simple built-up constructions. The whole could then be plastered over (or parts only plastered over) to yield a uniform, rigid surface which can be sanded down quite smooth.

Mould Finish

Regardless of the materials used for the construction of a plug, or a direct mould, this question of finishing glass-smooth with a fully sealed surface is all-important. A GRP lay-up will faithfully duplicate any defects in the surface. Any porosity in the mould surface will encourage penetration of resin, even if apparently protected by

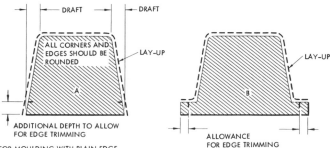

(A)   PATTERN FOR MOULDING WITH PLAIN EDGE
(B)   PATTERN FOR MOULDING WITH ROUNDED EDGE

FIG. 10.4

the parting agent applied. At best, this will produce a rough surface on the moulding in this area. At worse, the moulding will stick.

Plugs or moulds made from porous materials—e.g. wood or plaster—need the surface *thoroughly* sealing and preferably also given a high gloss varnish finish. Sealing will not only prevent soaking up gel coat resin but will also prevent any moisture present in the mould being drawn into the resin during lay-up and inhibiting cure.

Shapes are Important

The shape of the pattern must also take into account the fact that any GRP moulding taken off it will be rigid. Thus a male pattern should have draft or taper on the vertical surfaces so that the moulding does not become locked in place—Fig. 10.4. It should also be of sufficient extra size to allow for the fact that the edges of a GRP lay-up will be starved of resin, and relatively weak. They must therefore come outside the final shape. Similar considerations apply in the case of a female pattern. Where the pattern is used as a plug, of course, a male pattern produces a female mould and a female pattern a male mould.

If it is strictly necessary to accommodate reverse tapers or undercuts in the pattern, then the mould derived must be split. Some examples are shown in Fig. 10.5. Split moulds are to be avoided, whenever

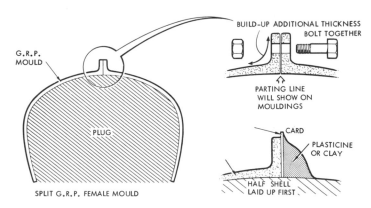

SPLIT G.R.P. FEMALE MOULD

FIG. 10.5

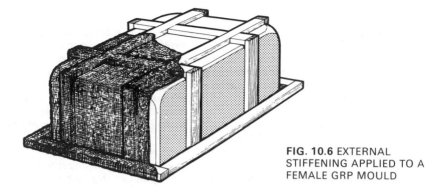

FIG. 10.6 EXTERNAL
STIFFENING APPLIED TO A
FEMALE GRP MOULD

possible, especially in amateur construction.

Where the pattern is to be used to produce a GRP mould, provision should be made on the plug to ensure that the edges of the mould are flanged. This will add considerable stiffness to the mould, as well as making it easier to remove mouldings from the mould itself. In the case of a female mould, too, a flanged edge allows an extra depth of moulding to be produced to offset the natural tendency for the top part of a moulding to taper down in thickness when consolidated. This extra lip of moulding is then cut off when the moulding has cured and has been removed from the mould.

It is well worth while to bring the plug up to the highest finish possible, so that the finish obtained on the surface of the GRP mould will be as near perfect as possible. Whilst surface defects on the GRP mould can be smoothed and polished out, this is a lengthy and tedious process. It is much better to eliminate the necessity for such re-working by putting the extra time necessary into finishing the *plug* to achieve perfection of finish.

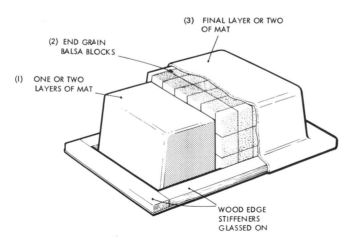

(3) FINAL LAYER OR TWO
OF MAT

(2) END GRAIN
BALSA BLOCKS

(I) ONE OR TWO
LAYERS OF MAT

WOOD EDGE
STIFFENERS
GLASSED ON

FIG. 10.7 FEMALE GRP MOULD WITH BUILT-IN STIFFENERS (Sandwich construction)

A GRP Mould

A GRP mould is laid up on a plug in a similar manner to any GRP construction. About the only difference is that a slightly thicker gel coat should be used—0.020-0.025in (0,5-0,6mm) thick or approximately 2 ounces (600g/m²) of resin per sq. ft. A fast-setting resin should be used for preference. Moulds with large vertical surfaces should use a thixotropic resin to prevent draining. Once the gel coat has set, a layer of surface tissue should be applied with resin, followed by succeeding layers of glass fibre mat to build up to a suitable thickness.

The thickness required obviously depends on the size of the mould. As a rough rule, work to a thickness of 1½ times that which would be considered suitable for the actual *moulding* (to be taken off the mould). It need not be any thicker than that, for extra stiffness and rigidity can be given by adding bracing strips, etc., to the outside of the mould, in the manner shown in Fig. 10.6. A further way of stiffening a GRP mould without the expense of ad-ditional mat layers or the addition of external stiffeners is to use balsa blocks in 'sandwich' construction—Fig. 10.7.

It is very important that a GRP mould should be rigid enough to resist distortion or bending when removed from the plug. It must be absolutely 'solid', so that it maintains the shape of the plug faithfully when removed from it, and when being worked on in using it as a mould to produce a lay-up moulding. This means anticipating the amount of external reinforcement necessary whilst the GRP mould is still on the plug. All such reinforcement should be added, and the mould *left* on the plug, *until fully cured and hardened.* In the case of a moulding where the shape is critical, this means a minimum of two days, unless post-curing can be applied, (e.g. applying heat from a hot-air blower).

This chapter has treated the subject of moulds generally. Moulds are essentially individual to particular jobs, and so further information on this subject will be found in further chapters dealing with specific constructions.

CHAPTER ELEVEN

Hand lay-up

The same basic technique applies in all hand lay-up of 'contact' mouldings—so-called because the resin/glass fibre is laid up in contact with the mould, without the application of pressure, other than that used to consolidate the glass fibre reinforcement and ensure that it is thoroughly wetted.

Several stages are involved which may be summarised as follows:—

(i) Choice of suitable materials—the majority of GRP work is done with chopped strand mat and general purpose resin, but see also chapters 3 and 4 for more specific information on different types of reinforcement and resins, respectively.

(ii) Estimating and obtaining quantities required—see chapter 7.

(iii) Preparation of the mould.

(iv) Application of gel coat.

(v) Mixing of laminating resin and completion of lay-up.

(vi) Leaving the finished laminate in the mould to cure.

Preparing the Mould

The mould must be clean (removing any remaining parting agent if the mould has been used before), free from surface damage, grease or dust, etc.

Initially, at least, recommended treatment is to apply three coats of wax polish at about 6-hour intervals, followed by treatment with release agent. For subsequent use a single coat of wax polish will generally be adequate.

Apply release agent *sparingly* either by spray (two mist coats) or brush, otherwise it will take too long to dry, especially if it drains into pools. The release agent *must* be left to dry thoroughly otherwise it will not form a proper skin and the moulding will stick.

Working Conditions

Ideally the air temperature should be *at least* 50°F (10°C). If the temperature is lower than this, 4% catalyst (hardener) should be used, or 'winter additive'. If the temperature is below about 40°F (5°C) however, it is best to leave laying-up until conditions improve, or the area can be heated. 'Winter additives' can promote gelling and setting in cold air, but the resulting moulding may suffer as a consequence because of incomplete curing.

More important still—the air should be dry, or reasonably dry. Never attempt laying-up in damp or excessively humid conditions as the moisture in the air will inhibit setting of the resin. This cannot be compensated for by chemical additives.

The Gel Coat

For this, a *gel coat* resin must be used. If a self-coloured moulding is required, this is normally added to the gel coat only. The gel coat resin is thus prepared by mixing

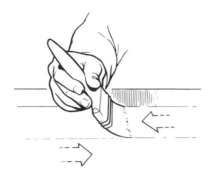

FIG. 11.1 PAINT ON GEL COAT WITH CONTINUOUS MOTION (Do not paint backwards and forwards)

with a suitable pigment paste, avoiding the formation of air bubbles. Any pigment added must be dispersed thoroughly in the resin.

Note: If identical colour matching is required on two or more mouldings, enough coloured gel coat resin to do *all* the mouldings involved should be made up at the same time. Separate quantities of this basic colour mix can then be used, as required.

After activating with catalyst (hardener) the resin should be brushed in place, using a wide, soft brush and single, sweeping strokes. The aim should be to get an even distribution of resin in one continuous application, not brushing backwards and forwards (Fig. 11.1). In the case of near horizontal surfaces, the resin can often be poured in place and distributed with a brush. The aim should be to achieve a uniform gel coat thickness of between 0.01 and 0.02 in (0.25-0.5 mm). If a lambs-wool paint roller is used to distribute the gel coat over large surfaces, it will be impossible to produce this thickness in a single coat. In that case the first coat should be left to gel, and second coat then applied. No attempt should be made to paint or roll over a first coat of resin until it has gelled or set to a condition where it is no longer sticky to the touch. Equally, avoid touching a gel coat which has not

gelled, as this will fingerprint it. Test with the finger on an area which will subsequently be cut off the moulding when trimming to final shape.

No further work can be done in the mould until the gel coat has gelled, or set to the point where it is like a fairly rigid jelly with no surface tackiness.

The Laminating Resin

The accelerator is commonly mixed with the resin, as supplied (pre-accelerated resin). If not, it should be added to the resin first in the recommended proportion.

In the particular cases where fillers or pigments are to be used, these should be added next and thoroughly dispersed by complete mixing, but avoiding excessive agitation which could introduce air bubbles into the resin. If necessary, the resin should be left to stand until clear of air bubbles.

The exception to this rule is where an absorbent filler is used, e.g. sawdust. In this case the resin should be activated with catalyst before the filler is added and mixed in. This will ensure proper distribution of the catalyst through the resin. If the catalyst is added last, the filler will show a preferential absorption for the catalyst, which may starve the resin of catalyst and result in an incomplete cure.

The catalyst (hardener) should only be

added immediately before the resin is required for use. Once added, the resin will have a strictly limited pot life. The proportion of catalyst is not critical, but use recommended quantities. Lacking any specific information on the subject, a 3% proportion of catalyst (by weight) can be considered suitable for general use. This may be increased to 4% to produce a faster gelling time, e.g. if the temperature is low, or decreased to 2% to lengthen the gelling time, if the temperature is high. If the temperature is very low, then additional catalyst or 'winter additive' should be used, in proportions specified by the supplier.

Working Procedure

After the gel coat has set—and not before—mix up a sufficient quantity of laminating resin and hardener for the job. This is normally clear resin, although pigment may be added for 'through' colour if thought desirable. Fillers should *not* be used in the laminating or lay-up resin.

A coating of resin is painted over the gel coat, followed by laying the glassfibre in place. The first layer may be of glass tissue, to serve as a 'screen' to mask the glass pattern in subsequent layers, but the use of surfacing tissue is largely a matter of personal preference. If not used, proceed directly with the first layer of mat (or cloth).

This should be cut or torn to suitable size, laid in place over the wet resin and stippled down in place with a stiff brush, using a *dabbing* motion only. Avoid sweeping or 'painting' strokes, as this will only pull up the glass fibres, particularly in the case of mat. Dabbing down can be

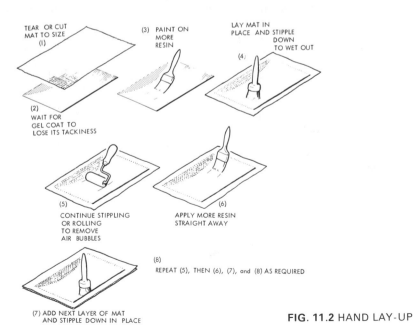

(1) TEAR OR CUT MAT TO SIZE

(2) WAIT FOR GEL COAT TO LOSE ITS TACKINESS

(3) PAINT ON MORE RESIN

(4) LAY MAT IN PLACE AND STIPPLE DOWN TO WET OUT

(5) CONTINUE STIPPLING OR ROLLING TO REMOVE AIR BUBBLES

(6) APPLY MORE RESIN STRAIGHT AWAY

(7) ADD NEXT LAYER OF MAT AND STIPPLE DOWN IN PLACE

(8) REPEAT (5), THEN (6), (7), and (8) AS REQUIRED

FIG. 11.2 HAND LAY-UP

followed by rolling to ensure proper consolidation and wetting of the glass. The two important things to ensure are:-

(i) All the glass is thoroughly wetted with resin. This will be shown by the change of colour of the glass from whitish to a translucent look. Make sure that no white patches remain.

(ii) The glass reinforcement is properly tamped down with *no air bubbles* trapped in or under it. It is *very important* that any air bubbles are removed as these will otherwise form weak spots in the moulding.

Glass fibre mat will mould readily to curved shapes, although it may prove difficult to bed down properly over sharper curves. It may be best in such areas to shred the mat before laying in place, to provide looser fibres which can be bedded down.

Opinion tends to differ on the matter of joints, where one piece of glass fibre has to carry on from another. To ensure maximum joint strength it is best to overlap the next piece over the first by about 1½ in to 2 in (35 to 50 mm) and then work over this overlap to spread the two layers out to a uniform thickness (Fig. 11.3). Again this is easier if the second edge is shredded slightly first. Somewhat neater results can be produced by laying the second piece of glass fibres together to intermesh. This is a trickier operation, and there is a danger of thinning the reinforcement along the joint line. As a consequence the moulding will be weaker at this point because of the higher resin content. This can be offset to a large extent by making sure that joints in subsequent layers occur in different places.

Succeeding layers of glass reinforcement can be laid up, in turn, directly on the first whilst the resin is still wet, i.e. there is no need to let the first layer gel before applying the next. In fact, it is better to work through all the layers continuously, as this will produce the most homogeneous moulding.

The exception is where a large number of layers are being used. Four layers of 1½ ounce (450g/m²) mat (or more specifically, 6 ounces (1800g m²) of glass reinforcement per square foot) is about the maximum thickness which can be laid up directly, one on top of the other, without the moulding becoming excessively hot. With thick mouldings, therefore, lamination should be stopped at this stage until the first layers have gelled and hardened off. Further build-up can then be attempted without fear of possible overheating and damage to the gel coat (Fig. 11.4).

Similar considerations apply when ribs, stiffeners or similar sections are to be added to a moulding. The moulding should be left to harden off before these are added and glassed on. This will ensure that the moulding is rigid enough to resist possible distortion.

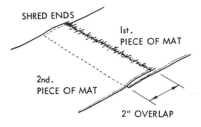
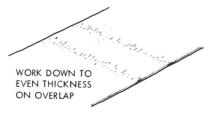

SHRED ENDS

1st. PIECE OF MAT

2nd. PIECE OF MAT

2" OVERLAP

WORK DOWN TO EVEN THICKNESS ON OVERLAP

FIG. 11.3 BASIC JOINT TECHNIQUE

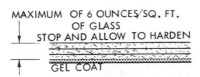

FIG. **11**.4 MAXIMUM THICKNESS FOR CONTINUOUS WET LAY-UP

The Final Surface

In a majority of cases the 'last' surface is left as stippled or rolled in place. The appearance may however, be improved by the final addition of surface tissue applied on the 'wet' lay-up, rolling down in the usual way. A final 'gel coat' of plain resin can then be added further to improve the surface appearance, but using the laminating resin for this (not a gel coat resin).

Removal from the Mould

The moulding must be left in the mould for a suitable time to mature properly, so that it can be removed without fear of distortion–see chapter 5. Even in the case of non-critical mouldings, allow at least 24 hours and preferably twice that time.

It is unlikely, even with a generous application of parting agent, that the moulding will lift easily out of the mould. Usually it will have to be released first by prising away from the sides of the mould. For this job a putty knife or similar tool with a thin flat flexible blade can be useful, but with the edges blunted to avoid scratching either the mould or the moulding. The blade should be worked between the mould and the moulding, and then along, working around the edge. Sometimes it may be necessary to work right round the edge before the moulding becomes free. In other cases, it may free itself almost immediately. There is also the chance that it will stick completely and not come free! In

that case, it is a matter of working on freeing it with minimum damage to the mould and moulding– or sacrificing one to save the other, so that a new start can be made.

If it Sticks in the Mould

If it sticks in the mould, then you probably have not given enough attention to mould surface preparation. But you still stand a good chance of getting it out. Try using shallow hardwood wedges tapped lightly between the moulding and the mould to prise it away. Having lifted it to some extent, water poured between the mould and moulding to dissolve the release agent (if a water soluble type) can further help release. Then further prise the moulding away from the mould until it breaks free.

Finally, check what went wrong, so that you do not have the same trouble next time.

Is the Moulding Cured?

A simple test to check whether a moulding which has been removed from the mould is cured or not is to tap over its surface with a coin to hear if it 'rings'. If so, all is well. On the other hand, if tapping produces a 'dead' sound, then the moulding has not yet cured. If possible, replace it in the mould to continue curing with minimum risk of distortion. If left to cure out of the

FIG. 11.5 HAND LAY-UP MOULDING STEPS

1. Polishing the mould

2. Applying release agent

3. Applying gel coat resin

mould it could distort appreciably by the time it has fully set.

The scientific method of checking whether or not a moulding has cured is to measure its *hardness* with a Barcol impressor. Basically, however, this only gives a comparative figure. A reference value is established by measuring the Barcol hard-

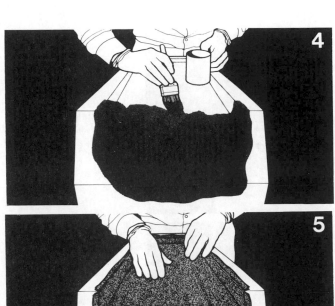

4. Laminating resin applied generously over cured gel coat

5. First layer of glass mat smoothed into position

6. Mat rollered down to produce complete impregnation with resin, removing all air bubbles. (Stages 4, 5 and 6 then repeated for each layer of mat)

ness of a known fully cured laminate. Any lower value determined for further laminates then indicates the (comparative) degree of under-cure.

Cured hardness will also depend to some extent on the type of resin used. Using a type 934/1 impressor for a Barcol hardness test, for example, the hardness of

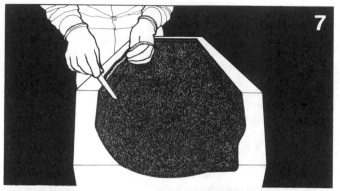

7. Edge of finished laminate may be trimmed with a sharp knife whilst still 'green' (i.e. not fully set. Alternatively, edge trimming is done with a hacksaw or bandsaw after moulding has set and has been removed from mould)

8. If necessary, edges of moulding are prised away from mould.

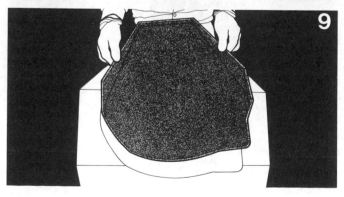

9. Moulding is then lifted out of mould

(Illustrations by British Industrial Plastics Ltd)

fully cured, reinforced polyester resin will normally fall into the range 80-90. Anything less than about half these values would almost certainly indicate under-cured resin.

CHAPTER TWELVE

Simple moulded shapes

Only simple moulds are required for producing 'tray' shapes, which are usually most effectively constructed from wood on a hardboard or ply base. Where the 'tray' is to have a smooth inner surface a male mould is required. Here the basic shape or pattern can be cut from wood block, or a simple built-up box, secured to a base-panel (Fig. 12.1). All four bottom corners should be generously radiused.

If the 'tray' is to have a plain edge, then the depth of the mould needs to be approximately 1 in deeper than the final form to allow for trimming off. If the 'tray' edge is to be lipped or flanged, then the pattern height is obviously actual size, but the sharp edge should be reduced with the aid of a fillet, as shown in the detail sketches. A further improvement is to build up a separate frame around the basic form,

with generous fillets, to produce a rolled-over or beaded edge on the final moulding.

Simple stiffeners are readily incorporated in the mould. Longitudinal stiffeners can be used on medium sizes. These need to be the same depth, and parallel, if the tray is to stand on the base. Larger tray shapes are more effectively braced with diagonal stiffeners. Filleting of the base of stiffeners should not be necessary, provided their depth is kept quite small. Stiffeners added in this way to the mould, of course, produce hollow sections in the base of the final moulding. If raised sections are required—e.g. for photographic dishes—the sections would have to be hollowed out of the base of the mould.

Where the 'outside' surface of the tray is required to be smooth, a female mould can be constructed from a simple wood frame

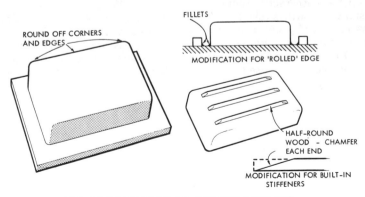

ROUND OFF CORNERS AND EDGES

FILLETS

MODIFICATION FOR 'ROLLED' EDGE

HALF-ROUND WOOD - CHAMFER EACH END

MODIFICATION FOR BUILT-IN STIFFENERS

FIG. 12.1 MALE MOULD FOR TRAY SHAPES

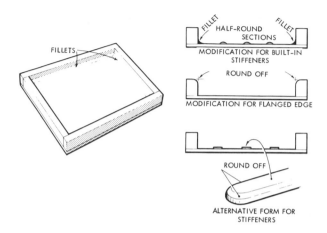

FILLETS

FILLET FILLET
HALF-ROUND
SECTIONS

MODIFICATION FOR BUILT-IN
STIFFENERS

ROUND OFF

MODIFICATION FOR FLANGED EDGE

ROUND OFF

ALTERNATIVE FORM FOR
STIFFENERS

FIG. 12.2 FRAME MOULD FOR TRAY SHAPES

laid out on a ply or hardboard base. Fillets are more difficult, although these can be formed in plasticine. No draft or taper is necessary for one-off mouldings, even with deep tray sections, as if the moulding sticks the original framework can be broken away to release the moulding.

Lipped edges are easy to accommodate. Stiffening sections can be added directly to the base of the mould. If reverse sections are required, these can be produced by building up the base section with wide strips, as shown in the detail sketches (Fig. 12.2). Two layers of $1\frac{1}{2}$ (450g/m²) ounce mat should be adequate for tray sizes up to about 24-30 inches (largest dimension). An additional layer can be used on larger

mouldings, or where extra rigidity is required.

Some uses of tray shapes:

Photographic dishes.

Domestic trays (note shapes may be circular or elliptic as well as rectangular).

Complete tabletops (smooth side up, with suitable lip. If stiffening is required, separate stiffeners should be bonded to the underside, or sandwich construction can be used (see chapter 20).

Small parts containers and cutlery holders. (Divisions can be cut from moulded flat sheet, bonded in place with resin only).

5° MINIMUM DRAFT

ALLOW 1"
EXTRA DEPTH
FOR CUT EDGE

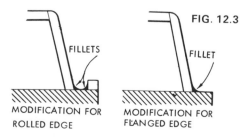

FIG. 12.3

FILLETS

FILLET

MODIFICATION FOR
ROLLED EDGE

MODIFICATION FOR
FLANGED EDGE

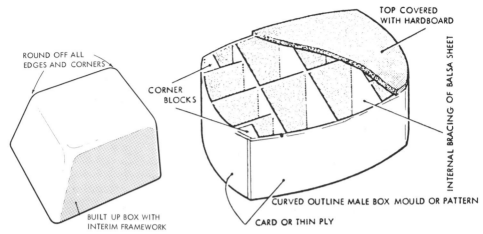

ROUND OFF ALL
EDGES AND CORNERS

CORNER
BLOCKS

BUILT UP BOX WITH
INTERIM FRAMEWORK

TOP COVERED
WITH HARDBOARD

INTERNAL BRACING OF BALSA SHEET

CURVED OUTLINE MALE BOX MOULD OR PATTERN

CARD OR THIN PLY

FIG. 12.4 MALE MOULD FOR BASIC BOX SHAPES

FIG. 12.5

Lids.

Seed boxes (perforations can be drilled in after moulding).

Rigid covers.

Draining boards.

Refrigerator and icebox liners.

Cupboard shelves.

Box Forms

Male moulds for producing box mouldings with smooth inner surfaces can be built up from ply or hardboard sides with a thicker wood top. Bracing pieces should be incorporated in each corner so that all corners, and base edges, can be generously rounded off. At least 5 degrees draft is recommended on the sides to make for easy removal of the moulding from the mould (Fig. 12.3). Stiffening sections may or may not be needed on the sides and/or base, depending on the size of the box and its intended function.

Female moulds need construction with external strutting (Fig. 10.6). A slightly more generous draft is required, unless only one moulding is required, when the mould can be broken down to release. Filleting of the bottom edge of the mould is a little more difficult because of the limited access, as is

smoothing and finishing the mould surface. If a particularly good outer surface finish is required from the moulding, in fact, it is probably better to make a male mould, and from this a GRP female mould, even for a one-off job.

For making identical, but 'handed' boxes, one male mould should be constructed. A GRP moulding is taken off this to form the matching female mould. Further mouldings taken off each of these two will then provide handed pairs of mouldings.

Shapes can, of course, readily be varied when making the original patterns, in which case thick card may take the place of ply or hardboard for curved sides in the construction of a male mould (Fig. 12.5). Interior bracing can be used to support the sides to the necessary curvature, as required. Balsa sheet is a convenient material for such strutting, because of the ease with which it can be cut to shape and assembled with quick-drying balsa cement.

Large boxes can easily be built up from moulded flat sheet panels, avoiding the construction of large moulds, although simple jigs may be needed to hold the individual panels in place whilst jointing. Some possible edge joints are shown in Fig. 12.6. Choice of edge joint used depends

75

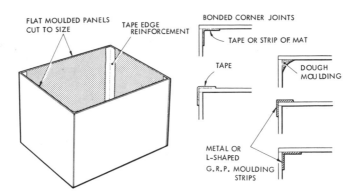

FLAT MOULDED PANELS
CUT TO SIZE

TAPE EDGE
REINFORCEMENT

BONDED CORNER JOINTS

TAPE OR STRIP OF MAT

TAPE

DOUGH
MOULDING

METAL OR
L-SHAPED
G.R.P. MOULDING
STRIPS

FIG. 12.6 BUILT-UP BOXES

mainly on the size of the construction and its purpose. Mechanical fastening is often an advantage, alternative to, or allied to, bonding with resin and resin/glass. In the latter case mechanical fastenings will hold the assembly in place whilst the resin is setting.

Some uses of mould boxes (note: lids can be matching 'boxes' or 'trays', attached with metal hinges):

Toolboxes.
Containers.
Cases.
Luggage.
Cloches.
Panniers.
Caravan bodies.
Dog kennels (inverted box with cutout 'door.).
Battery boxes.
Wheelbarrows.
Tanks.
Ducts (long boxes with open ends).
Sidecars.
Cabinets.
Trailer bodies.
Trucks.

Shell Mouldings

Shell mouldings normally have to be made as two separate handed halves, sub-

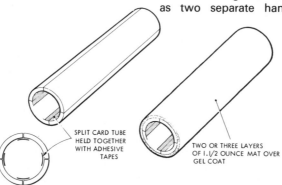

SPLIT CARD TUBE
HELD TOGETHER
WITH ADHESIVE
TAPES

TWO OR THREE LAYERS
OF 1.1/2 OUNCE MAT OVER
GEL COAT

FIG. 12.7 CYLINDRICAL MOULDINGS (See also Fig. 12.13)

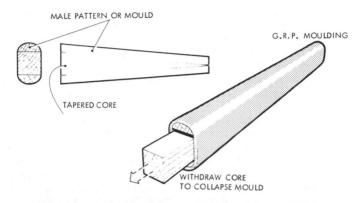

MALE PATTERN OR MOULD

G.R.P. MOULDING

TAPERED CORE

WITHDRAW CORE
TO COLLAPSE MOULD

FIG. 12.8 STRAIGHT TAPERED SHELL MOULDINGS

sequently joined to complete the shell. The exception is a purely cylindrical shell when a single pattern can be used as a male mould–e.g. a length of card tube, as shown in Fig. 12.7. To facilitate removal of the tube after the moulding has been laid up on it, the tube should be prepared by slitting carefully down its length to make two or three separate sections, which are then rejoined with masking tape on the inside. After the moulding is completed and has hardened, the masking tape strips can be pulled off through the inside of the tube,

when it should be possible to spring the card tube sections apart and withdraw them.

A similar technique can be applied to straight tapered shell shapes. In this case a male mould is constructed around a tapered core piece, as shown in Fig. 12.8, held in place with a locking plate at each end. After the lay-up is complete the locking plates are removed and the core piece withdrawn. The outer pieces of the mould can then be sprung free and withdrawn.

Since both of these methods utilise a

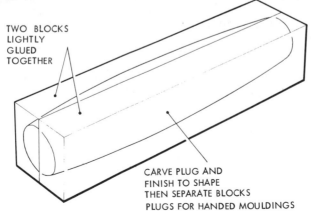

TWO BLOCKS
LIGHTLY
GLUED
TOGETHER

CARVE PLUG AND
FINISH TO SHAPE
THEN SEPARATE BLOCKS
PLUGS FOR HANDED MOULDINGS

FIG. 12.9

male mould, the shell mouldings are of smooth bore, but with a rough outer surface. Shell mouldings with a smooth outer surface require the use of handed female moulds, each producing a half shell. In this case a plug is constructed first, then separated down the middle, and a female GRP mould laid up on each.

A plug for splitting should be made up from two separate, but identical, blocks or sub-assemblies which are only lightly joined together. This will enable them to be worked as one, for final shaping, but easily separated along the true centreline (Fig. 12.9). Further additions must then be made to these two half shell patterns, according to the method to be used for joining the half shell mouldings.

If a butt joint is to be used, then each pattern must be extended to provide extra 'width' of moulding, so that it can be trimmed back to a clean edge (Fig. 12.10). A bonded joint of this type needs very accurate trimming of the cut edge of each moulding, if a perfect joint is to be obtained. The joint can be strengthened with glass tape applied on the inside of the assembly, as shown, provided this joint line is accessible. For straight butt joints it may be desirable to increase the thickness of the moulding locally in the region of the edge, which can be done quite simply when laying up in the female mould. No modification of the pattern is required for this.

Gaps in a butt joint can also be filled with resin/filler. If the moulding is coloured, then colour matching is important when gap filling. The same pigment paste used in resin/filler will need careful matching for shade. Pigmented (but not activated) resin saved from the original gel coating will not give a match when mixed with filler powder

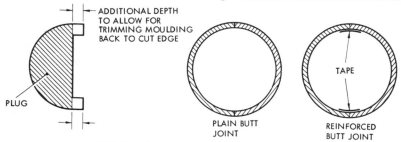

FIG. 12.10 HALF SHELL PLUGS AND SHELL

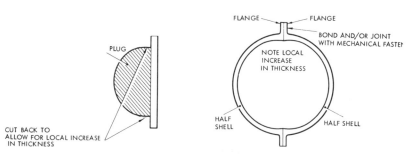

FIG. 12.11 FLANGED HALF SHELLS

MOULDING

SPRING
OFF

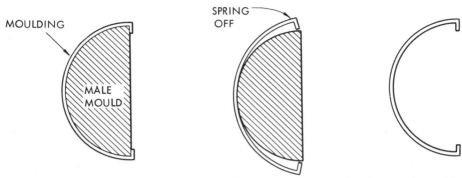

MALE
MOULD

FIG. 12.12 HALF SHELLS—With turned-in flange can only be produced on a male mould

because of the whitening effect of the latter, unless of course the colour is white to start with.

Flanged joints are much stronger and easier to fit up, but not always acceptable from the point of view of appearance. Some modification of the pattern is needed to allow for local thickening, and the formation of the flange—see Fig. 12.11.

Turned-in flanges are not a practical proposition for moulding with the shell although they can be produced if the shell is flexible enough to be sprung out of the mould (Fig. 12.12). The main difficulty then is getting a 'sharp' edge in the inside corner, which is the least accessible when laying up, and the most visible when the shells are joined. If turned-in flanges are to be used, they are best added as separate sections after the moulded shells have been removed from the female mould.

Various other methods of joining half shells neatly and effectively can often be devised, depending on the size and shape involved. Such problems present a challenge to individual ingenuity.

Some uses for Shell mouldings:
Pipes and ducts.
Model aircraft fuselages.
Streamlined or rounded form tanks.
Coalhods (tapered cylindrical shell with separately fitted end moulding).

Some uses for Half Shells (made directly off a male pattern; or from a female mould taken off a male pattern, depending on which is to be the smooth side):
Scooter legshields.
Machine guards.
Cloches.
Fairings.
Reflectors.
Shades.

Polyester resin with glass fibre reinforcement is particularly successful for making pipes and ducting of various kinds. The ease with which it can be formed into complex pipe shapes with difficult junctions, and the fact that it is resistant to most acids and alkalis, in addition to being proof against more ordinary substances such as oil and water, makes it a good choice for such work.

Straight lengths of pipe can be made round split mandrels by wrapping with strips of cloth or tape impregnated with resin. A simple example of this is shown in Fig. 12.13.

Larger diameter pipes can also be made inside a length of metal tube by placing glass mat, cut to overlap slightly, inside the tube; then pouring in a quantity of resin and rotating the tube rapidly, so that the centrifugal force causes the resin to impregnate the mat. Heat applied to the outside of the

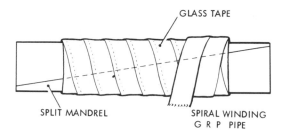

GLASS TAPE

SPLIT MANDREL

SPIRAL WINDING
G R P PIPE

FIG. 12.13

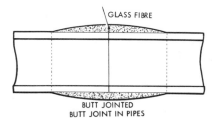

GLASS FIBRE

BUTT JOINTED
BUTT JOINT IN PIPES

FIG. 12.14

tube assists the curing process, and subsequent release is relatively easy, as the moulding shrinks away from the metal tube.

Pipes with simple bends in them can be made on the outside of flexible moulds such as plastic tubing and 'Vinamold' mouldings. Although the resin shrinks on to the mould and tends to grip it, release is reasonably easy if the mould is sufficiently flexible. The resin impregnated tape or cloth wrapped round the former can be kept in close contact, and given a tidier surface, if it is wrapped with strips of cellophane. Failing this, it is essential not to allow too much free resin on the surface of the cloth,as it tends to gather in blobs and give a poor appearance.

Ducting of a complex shape can be formed over a mould made of a material with a low melting point, when, after the laminate has cured, it can be heated in an oven and the mould melted out. Paraffin wax and some of the special fusible metal alloys are suitable for this kind of job.

Pipes or ducts can be joined together simply and effectively by butt joining them and binding with several turns of glass tape impregnated with resin (Fig. 12.14). The ends to be joined should be first cleaned thoroughly by scraping or by sanding. When the resin sets it contracts sufficiently to make a very firm joint.

Emergency repairs to burst water pipes can be successfully made in the manner described above, although it is as well to remember that burst pipes usually occur in cold weather in cold places and it is best to apply some local heat to the joint to ensure that the resin cures properly.

CHAPTER THIRTEEN

Casting, potting and encapsulation

Polyester resins with no reinforcement will solidify on curing to a clear, transparent solid. Although this will not be as strong as a reinforced material its mechanical properties are quite adequate for many applications—notably the production of decorative 'glassfibre' articles, embedding of specimens, and the encapsulation of electrical components.

Strictly speaking there is a difference between *casting* and *potting*. A casting is made in a removable mould, so a number of identical castings can be made from the same mould. Potting, on the other hand, refers to the resin being 'cast' in an outer shell which subsequently becomes part of the final product. The technique is otherwise identical.

Embedding then refers to the process of enclosing specimens or other objects completely in a clear block *casting*. Not only does this ensure a completely homogeneous block of clear resin, but since polyester resins shrink appreciably on curing, the final form is more accurate. With potting, the cast resin will tend to shrink away from the casing used unless this is a material (such as polystyrene sheet) having good adhesion to the cast polyester and is thin-walled enough to follow the shrinkage of the resin on curing.

Encapsulation is the term given to the complete enclosure of an electric component or circuit or sub-circuit, etc., in a 'casting' of resin. In this case it does not normally matter whether it is produced as a true casting, or by potting. Also the final appearance does not need to be clear and transparent. Thus fillers can be used with the resin to reduce shrinkage and, rather more important, to help absorb and disperse the heat produced by the resin as it sets.

Gelation on setting of the resin is the result of an exothermic chemical reaction taking place which involves the evolution of an appreciable amount of heat. This exothermic heat must be dissipated quickly if internal stresses in the casting are to be avoided, resulting in cracking. Also, of course, if articles being embedded or encapsulated are heat-sensitive it is even more important to avoid excessive heat being developed during the resin setting stage. The various ways in which this heat can be controlled are:—

(i) Type and concentration of catalyst and accelerator.

(iii) Thickness or volume of casting curing at any one time.

(iv) Temperature at which gelation is initiated.

(v) Type and quantity of filler (if used).

(vi) Type of mould.

As far as (i) is concerned, choice is a *casting resin* of low reactivity (i.e. slow setting)—usually about 0.5% accelerator and 1 to 2% hardener. This is to ensure minimum exothermic heating during cold-curing, and minimum shrinkage. Ordinary resins can be adjusted for slow setting, but it is always preferable to use a special

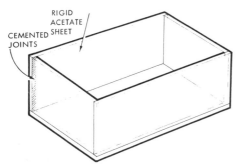

RIGID ACETATE SHEET
CEMENTED JOINTS

FIG. 13.1 HOLLOW BOX MOULD FOR CASTINGS

casting resin, which will also ensure a clear, glasslike colour with good optical properties. There are also various different types of casting resins. Some include up to 25% plasticizing or flexibilizing resin to give a less brittle, more resilient casting of equal clarity and may be preferred for embedding. They would not normally be used for encapsulation of electronic components, however, as they are less moisture resistant.

Simple Castings and Embedding

A suitable non-stick mould can be made from acetate sheet of sufficient thickness to be rigid—e.g. see Fig. 13.1. Other materials can, of course, also be used for making moulds—e.g. specially shaped moulds could be made from GRP—but will normally need treatment with release agent. For large, or deep, castings there can be advantages in using a metal mould as these will help dissipate exothermic heat.

For the embedding of specimens of insects, small sea creatures, shells, coins, etc.—or for decorative paperweights—clear resins are normally employed, with simple basic shapes.

The technique involved is quite simple. Enough resin should be prepared (with catalyst) to fill the mould to a depth of about $\frac{1}{2}$in. This should be left to gel and harden with the top of the mould covered to exclude dust. Another $\frac{1}{2}$in layer of new resin can then be added, and so on. Once suitable height has been built up, the specimen to be potted can be placed on the gelled resin layer, and the mould progressively filled with further layers (Fig. 13.2). The main things to avoid are:—

(i) Letting dust or foreign matter fall into the mould on to a layer of resin.

(ii) Touching or fingerprinting the soft gel surface.

(iii) Letting air bubbles become trapped in the resin when pouring each layer.

(iv) Pouring too deep a layer at one time, as this can lead to excessive heating (which could damage delicate specimens), and shrinking (which could cause cracks to appear).

(v) Pouring the next layer of resin before the first layer has hardened and cooled down.

When the whole block has hardened

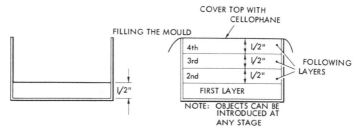

FILLING THE MOULD

1/2"

COVER TOP WITH CELLOPHANE

4th	1/2"
3rd	1/2"
2nd	1/2"
FIRST LAYER	

FOLLOWING LAYERS

NOTE: OBJECTS CAN BE INTRODUCED AT ANY STAGE

FIG. 13.2

completely, it can be removed from the mould. The surfaces can then be cleaned and polished to finish or even sawn or ground to a different shape and finally polished, preferably with a metal polish or jeweller's rouge and a buffing wheel in an electric drill.

Some slight tackiness may, however, be found on the top surface of the resin. If this shows up as a failing with the resin used it can be cured next time by covering the final surface with cellophane, strapped in place with cellulose tape, to exclude air.

Avoiding Air Bubbles

Certain objects need special care when being potted. If the object is flat, like a coin, then there is the possibility of trapping an air bubble underneath it when laying on the gelled layer. This can be avoided by pouring a little liquid resin on to the surface first and pressing and 'rocking' the coin down in place in this 'puddle' to remove any traces of air before proceeding with filling the next layer.

Specimens or objects which are likely to contain trapped air need a slightly different technique, adjusting the layers around the object so that complete immersion is achieved only after three or four separate layers have been poured. This will allow air to work up through the top part of the specimen and escape.

Treating Delicate Subjects

Where specimens being embedded are delicate and easily damaged by heat a slow-acting catalyst should be used. If a long gel and cure time can be tolerated the catalyst should be used without an accelerator, using not more than 4% catalyst down to 2% catalyst for large castings. The whole of the resin can then be poured at the same

time and allowed to cure at room temperature. The time taken to cure, however, can range from up to 48 hours for small castings, up to a week or more for large castings.

Embedding Damp Objects

Objects which are damp, or contain moisture, present a special problem. They need drying out or dehydrating completely to achieve entirely satisfactory results. If not, the moisture given out will inhibit setting of the resin and also produce a cloudiness in the casting.

If the specimen is such that it can be dried out in a warm atmosphere (e.g. by putting it in an airing cupboard) no particular problems should arise. The main trouble usually occurs with biological specimens, or subjects which naturally contain a lot of water and would be damaged or ruined by 'heat drying'.

If a biological specimen has been kept in a preserving fluid such as formalin or alcohol, for example, it just needs washing thoroughly in running water to remove all such fluid which would otherwise produce bubbles in the casting. The specimen should then be dried out on a piece of blotting paper as far as possible and then immersed in pure acetone for 5-10 minutes. It is then removed, dried out on blotting paper again, when it is ready for embedding.

It will still contain some water but the outer layer of water has now been replaced with acetone which will ensure compatability with the resin.

A more thorough treatment—after water washing to remove preserving fluid, where applicable—is to immerse the specimen successively in 30%, 50%, 70%, 90% and finally 100% alcohol. This will pro-

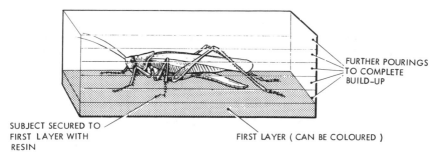

FURTHER POURINGS
TO COMPLETE
BUILD-UP

SUBJECT SECURED TO
FIRST LAYER WITH
RESIN

FIRST LAYER (CAN BE COLOURED)

FIG. 13.3 EMBEDDING A SUBJECT WHICH FLOATS IN RESIN

gressively replace all the water in the specimen with alcohol. After that the specimen is immersed in pure *acetone* to replace alcohol on the surface layer; then in a mixture of equal parts of acetone and *uncatalysed* resin, followed by a further dip in *uncatalysed* resin. It is then ready for embedding in low-activity *catalysed* resin with a long cure time.

Objects that Float

An additional problem arises when the object floats in the resin. Here it is necessary to hold the object down on the bottom layer of resin to avoid it floating out of place when the next layer is poured in. The simplest way of avoiding this is to use a tiny amount of resin to glue the object down to the gelled layer, letting this bond set before pouring on the next layer (Fig. 13.3).

Encapsulation

An exactly similar technique can be applied when potting or encapsulating functional objects, such as an electronic circuit. In this case, though, it is an advantage to mix a filler with the resin to reduce the amount of shrinkage.

Suitable fillers are mica, silicon flour, aluminium and calcium carbonate. The amount of filler used depends on the type and can range between 25% and 75% (although 20-30% by weight is a general working figure).

To obtain the best electrical properties from the resin it is also advisable to post-cure the casting by leaving in gentle heat (not more than 80°C) for a period of about ten to twelve hours.

A point to watch in encapsulating is that the resin (particularly if unfilled) can shrink away from lead-out wires and terminal inserts, opening up a path for the ingress of moisture. Precoating the leads with polythene is one way of avoiding this. An alternative method is post-coating with wax.

Decorative Castings

For making decorative and or functional castings the resin used can be clear, coloured with opaque or translucent pigments, or be mixed with fillers. Once again the resin should be of the slow-setting or 'casting' type, and in many cases may also be plasticised to reduce internal stresses when setting and eliminate cracking.

Moulds may be of rigid or flexible type. The latter are made from rubber-like materials, readily available, such as cold-curing silicone rubber and 'Vinamold' remeltable rubber. Cold-curing rubbers pro-

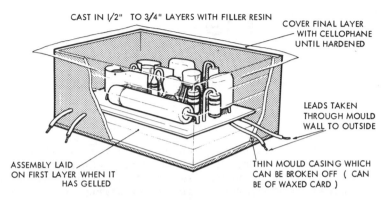

CAST IN 1/2" TO 3/4" LAYERS WITH FILLER RESIN

COVER FINAL LAYER WITH CELLOPHANE UNTIL HARDENED

LEADS TAKEN THROUGH MOULD WALL TO OUTSIDE

ASSEMBLY LAID ON FIRST LAYER WHEN IT HAS GELLED

THIN MOULD CASING WHICH CAN BE BROKEN OFF (CAN BE OF WAXED CARD)

FIG. 13.4 ENCAPSULATING AN ELECTRONIC CIRCUIT

duce durable, long-lasting moulds with fine reproduction of detail. The material cannot, however, be re-used. Remeltable rubbers are cheaper, and are particularly suited for making 'one off' or limited use moulds, with the advantage that the rubber can then be recovered (by melting down) and used again. The material also sets more quickly, so that a mould can be made ready for use in a minimum of time.

Neither type of flexible mould requires the use of release agents, although as a precaution they can be dusted with French chalk (which should then be smoothed out evenly over the mould surface) or coated with wax emulsion or PVA. Moulds in these materials are prepared by pouring the liquid rubber over a suitable pattern and then allowing to set in the form of a skin. After a suitable thickness has been built up, and the material has hardened, the rubber mould is stripped off the pattern. If necessary, large rubber moulds can be reinforced by bandage strip, scrim, or glass cloth, introduced as a reinforcing layer in building up the skin thickness. The pattern design should avoid undercuts and potential air pockets, and incorporate air vents or risers, if necessary, to prevent air being

trapped in the mould when the casting resin is poured in. Instructions for making suitable moulds, and limitations on shapes, are usually supplied with these moulding materials.

Casting is again usually best done in successive layers, the thickness of each layer depending primarily on the bulk of resin involved. It may be necessary to experiment to obtain the best results, and also adjust the proportion of fillers if necessary. It may, for example, be desirable to use a high proportion of fillers to minimise shrinkage and obtain fine detail reproduction, provided a more brittle casting is acceptable.

Possibilities with decorative castings are considerable, and by no means restricted to 'solid' forms. Other projects include decorative wall panels and wall sculptures, decorative glass panels and tabletops, etc. In other words, casting with polyester resin can be considered not only as a comparable production method to injection moulding, but also to decorative sheet forming in other types of sheet plastic. Large GRP panels, however, are usually more conveniently produced by hand lay-up moulding—see chapter 15.

CHAPTER FOURTEEN

GRP 'at home'

GRP can be used to make a wide variety of domestic articles, furniture, fittings, etc. Many of these are simple variations on the basic forms already described in chapter 12, or suitable combinations of these forms. The scope is enormous, but rather than thinking of copying existing articles in GRP it is best to think in terms of designing an article to perform the same function but utilises to the full the advantages offered by GRP, notably the freedom of shape and the ease with which curved forms can be produced. This will give the GRP object character, which at the same time can often disguise some of the limitations of GRP mouldings (e.g. the fact that they normally have a rough and a smooth side).

The following notes summarise specific requirements.

Draining Boards

With moulded-in ridges for draining, adequate stiffness should be given by two layers of $1\frac{1}{2}$ ounce ($450/m^2$) mat. Mouldings should be produced in a male mould similar to that for tray shapes (chapter 12) using a coloured gel coat backed up by a layer of glass tissue. A sealing coat of polyurethane varnish is an advantage.

Sinks

Produced on a male mould with sufficient draft for easy removal. Three layers of $1\frac{1}{2}$

ounce ($450g/m^2$) mat should be adequate, with a coloured gel coat backed by surface tissue. Polyurethane varnish can be used for sealing both surfaces. Drain and tap fittings can be moulded in or holes can be drilled out for the latter in the final moulding.

Coal Hods

Coal hods are usually best made in sections, bonded together, to which a separate hinged lid (tray shape) can be fitted. Three layers of $1\frac{1}{2}$ ounce ($450g/m^2$) mat are recommended with additional edge reinforcement of tape. Hod mouldings should be through-coloured (i.e. using pigmented resin throughout). Colours may differ, e.g. a dark 'decorative' colour for the gel coat, with black for the other colour. Shapes that can be used include parallel and straight tapered shells, and boxes with a separate 'tray' end, if necessary.

Lampshades

Glassfibre lampshades are virtually a subject on their own. They are normally made from a single layer of 1 ounce ($300g/m^2$) or $1\frac{1}{2}$ ounce ($450g/m^2$) mat, laid up around a suitable former such as a polythene bucket, plastic flowerpot, or similar article of suitable shape. Opaque and translucent colours can be used in the resin to eliminate the 'neutral' appearance of glass fibre.

Very much more attractive lamp-shades can be produced by first tacking a layer of thin coloured material to the former, either plain or patterned. The glass fibre mat is then laid up directly over this, the two layers bonding together with the resin (Fig. 14.1).

Polythene containers are generally excellent for formers since they can be obtained in a wide variety of sizes and shapes. Also they do not need a parting agent to be applied before laying up the shade. With all other materials, a parting agent should be applied to the surface in the usual way, as for moulds.

Further possibilities include the embedding of leaves or similar flat objects with a decorative or artistic appeal in the resin lay-up (underneath the glass mat). These can be stuck to the former with dabs of PVA adhesive (white glue).

Fittings for the finished lampshades are usually best added by piercing around the rim of the moulding and sewing the wire in place. This joint is then covered with decorative tape or binding, glued in place with PVA.

Garden Furniture

This is a classic example of where the curved forms and shapes readily produced by mouldings can be exploited to the full. Curved shapes will also add rigidity. The 'top' face is always made the smooth surface on garden furniture, i.e. the fronts of chairs and the tops of tables. Leg sections can be moulded into the main shape, or legs can be attached separately—see Fig. 14.2).

Two to three layers of $1\frac{1}{2}$ ounce ($450 g/m^2$) mat is usually sufficient for all mouldings, although local stiffening may be needed. Through colouring is generally advisable, except for translucent panels which may be used on tables. Alternatively the rough side of the finished moulding can be flock sprayed.

Household Repairs

Repairs to Water Tanks—see chapter 16.
Repairs to Coal Hods, Buckets and Similar Metal Containers.

This follows the same procedure as for water tanks, applying the glass fibre reinforcement in the form of a layer on the inside, after first cleaning the surface as well as possible. In particular, remove any traces of coal dust, etc., from the surface of a coal hod, as this may inhibit the setting of the resin. If the article is to carry dry substances it may be used as soon as the glass plastic has set hard. If intended for

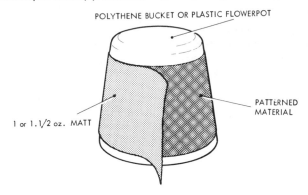

POLYTHENE BUCKET OR PLASTIC FLOWERPOT

1 or 1.1/2 oz. MATT

PATTERNED MATERIAL

FIG. 14.1

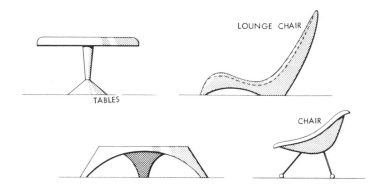

LOUNGE CHAIR

TABLES

CHAIR

FIG. 14.2

carrying water or other liquids it must be left to set for at least 48 hours for the laminate to set really hard and assume its maximum resistance to water absorption.

Repairs to Cisterns, etc.

Highly satisfactory and permanent repairs have been carried out on cisterns which have cracked following a freeze up, even where whole sections have been broken away. The broken parts are replaced—they can be glued back with resin—and then reinforced with a glass cloth or mat layer, as in the case of tanks, etc.

Repairs to Damaged Washbasins

Whilst repairs can be made to cracked washbasins by sticking the parts back with the resin and reinforcing the damaged area with a layer of glass cloth and resin applied from the underside, adhesion to the highly glazed surface is not always as satisfactory as it might be. Where a piece has been knocked right out of the basin and lost, the underside patch repair can be made and the basin filled up to a level surface again on the inside with resin/filler mix. This type of repair, however, can only be regarded as

a temporary remedy, although it will probably last for a considerable time.

Repairs to Gutters and Downpipes

Cracked or broken gutters, or those which have merely developed holes by corrosion are readily repaired with glass plastic. Preparation work required is to clean the inside of the gutter completely of loose corrosion products and make sure that it is perfectly dry. If necessary, use a blowlamp to dry out the damaged area before applying the resin.

If the area of damage is extensive, a mock-up former must be fitted around the gutter to give the repaired area the required shape. This can be done with cardboard which has been given a coat of wax polish, then bent to shape and held in position with clamps, string, wire, etc., as appropriate—see Fig. 14.3. Two layers of 1 or $1\frac{1}{2}$ ounce (300-450 g/m²) mat should provide adequate strength for a repair job of this nature.

In the case of broken downpipes, simply clean around the damaged area, coat generously with resin and lay on the glass mat (or cloth), stippling in position with a brush and more resin. When hard, the

FIG. 14.3

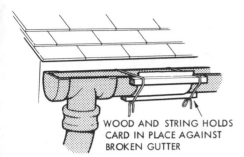

WOOD AND STRING HOLDS
CARD IN PLACE AGAINST
BROKEN GUTTER

edges can be cleaned up by filing, if necessary, and the repair work painted over.

Repairing Burst Pipes

The best material for repairing burst pipes is usually glass tape or cloth cut to appropriate widths. The pipe surface must first be cleaned with a wire brush and dried, as necessary, using a blowlamp to speed the drying time. Then apply a coat of resin, allowing at least an inch overlap each side of the crack, wind on the cloth strips or tape and thoroughly impregnate with a resin coat. Setting can be hastened by positioning an electric fire to warm the repair area, and must be complete—i.e. no surface tackiness apparent—before the water is turned on again and allowed to flow through the pipe.

This sort of repair is usually permanent as regards performance, but it is generally advisable to have a conventional repair made to the pipe later on, when convenient.

Reinforcing Fence Posts

It has been found that the life of fence posts can be materially improved by sheathing the bottom ends with a glass plastic layer before they are driven into the ground. This usually provides better 'pro-

ofing' than the usual method of coating with creosote, etc.

Repairs to Leaky Roofs

Stubborn leaks in garden sheds, caravan roof, boat cabin roofs, etc., can be sealed with a glass plastic 'patch' over the appropriate area, or by filling with resin/filler mix, depending on the circumstances and nature of the fault. Again, of course, such repair work can only be applied when the area concerned is perfectly dried out. Patch repairs, too, should be applied on the *outside*. The main trouble in many cases here is in deciding exactly where the water is getting in and which is the 'entry hole' that has to be sealed off.

Repairing Holes and 'Making Good'

An inexpensive 'mix' for repairing holes, fillling in cavities, etc., is a resin/sawdust mix compounded with the maximum amount of sawdust. This can be used for a wide variety of purposes where plaster, plastic wood, etc., might be considered as alternative materials and generally give a stronger bond and a better job. This type of mix can also be used effectively for filling in metal surfaces. In the case of large cavities to be filled, the bulk of the hollow space can be filled first with inexpensive bulk material, such as wood blocks, etc., and only the final surface repair done with the resin/filler mix.

CHAPTER FIFTEEN

Transparent and translucent panels

Polyester resins produced specifically for moulding translucent panels are clear resins with a refractive index as close as possible to that of glass. They are also tailored to have good resistance to ageing (i.e. resistance to discoloration by ultra violet light) and weathering. To achieve this, part of the styrene content is normally replaced with methyl methacrylate (and may be referred to as a *methacrylate* resin or *light stabilised* resin). They are normally used with special accelerators and a modified catalyst.

As far as the glass side is concerned, *powder-bonded* chopped strand mat is the preferred choice, but emulsion-bond mat can also be used.

Coloured translucent sheets are equally easy to produce, but the only suitable type of pigment is a *translucent colour paste.* Opaque colour pigments or pastes, however well thinned, will not produce satisfactory colour tinting.

Moulding technique for producing flat or corrugated sheets is extremely simple for no special moulds are required.

Flat Sheets

Any suitable smooth and flat surface will do as a mould, such as a sheet of new hardboard (used shiny side up). This should be several inches larger all round than the size of moulded panel required.

The hardboard panel should be covered with a single sheet of cellophane or polythene stretched in place, taut and free from wrinkles, taken around the edges and taped to the back with adhesive tape.

Cut glass mat to the required panel size. For small panels, a single piece of $1\frac{1}{2}$ ounce ($450\,g/m^2$) mat will be adequate. For medium size panels, a single piece of 2 ounce ($600\,g/m^2$) mat can be used. For large panels, two pieces of $1\frac{1}{2}$ ($450\,g/m^2$) ounce mat should be cut.

Mix up the resin, with or without pigment and paint a generous layer on to the cellophane or polythene covered hardboard surface. Lay the mat in place on top of the resin, making sure that it lies flat. Stipple in place lightly with a brush and then cover with a second sheet of cellophane or polythene (Fig. 15.1). Use a roller to consolidate the resin/glass and work out all traces of air bubbles. To provide a uniform and even smoother top surface a second piece of hardboard can be laid in place over the cellophane and the 'sandwich' further run over evenly with a roller. Remove this piece of hardboard and check that the panel appears sound throughout, viewing through the cellophane layer. Leave the cellophane in place until the resin has set and hardened. The top layer of cellophane can then be peeled off, and the moulded panel lifted off the cellophane covered hardboard.

Corrugated Panels

The moulding procedure is similar, except that corrugated sheeting (e.g. silica or iron) is used in place of hardboard. The

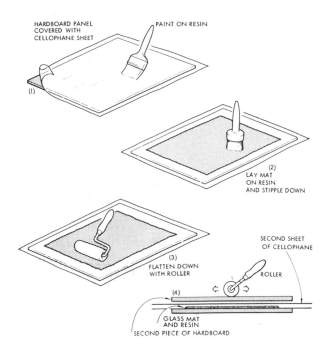

HARDBOARD PANEL
COVERED WITH
CELLOPHANE SHEET

PAINT ON RESIN

(1)

(2)
LAY MAT
ON RESIN
AND STIPPLE DOWN

(3)
FLATTEN DOWN
WITH ROLLER

SECOND SHEET
OF CELLOPHANE

ROLLER

(4)

GLASS MAT
AND RESIN
SECOND PIECE OF HARDBOARD

FIG. 15.1

width of glass mat needed to produce a required width of corrugated sheet can be found quite simply by running a piece of adhesive tape across the sheet, sticking to the corrugations (Fig. 15.2). Strip off, straighten out and measure the corresponding 'flat' width.

The corrugated sheet pattern is again covered with a single sheet of cellophane (or polythene) draped in position. This should be generously oversize in width to allow it to be drawn down into the corrugations and still leave some spare area each side. Paint resin directly on to the cellophane and follow up with the glass mat. This is then pressed and rolled down in place. Again a covering with a second sheet of cellophane followed by placing an identical piece of corrugated sheet over the

top and pressing down can be used to form the final shape, once all air bubbles have been removed by stippling.

If difficulty is experienced in laying the glass fibre in place and forming it into the corrugations, an alternative technique can be tried. Lay the first cellophane sheet out on a flat surface (e.g. a piece of hardboard), first making sure that the cellophane is wide enough for the job. Paint resin on the flat cellophane and lay the glass mat on top, stippling down until thoroughly wetted. Then transfer cellophane and resin to the corrugated sheet for final forming.

Panel edges should not be trimmed to shape until the sheet has fully hardened. The panel can then be cut to final size with a hacksaw or metal saw.

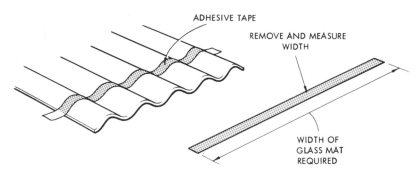

FIG. 15.2 MEASURE THE 'FLAT' WIDTH OF CORRUGATED SHEET

Some uses for Flat Sheets:

Small rooflight panes.
'Unbreakable' windows for garden sheds, etc.
Obscure window panes.
'Stained glass' window panes (translucent colours).
Heat resistant mats.
Heat-resistant tabletops.
Decorative 'see-through' table tops.

Built-up box constructions.
Shelves (with added stiffeners).
Lightweight doors (with added stiffeners).
Garage doors (from separate panels, joined).

Some uses for Corrugated Sheets:

Rooflights.
Roofing for garden rooms, sheds, outhouses, garages, etc.
Patio windbreaks.

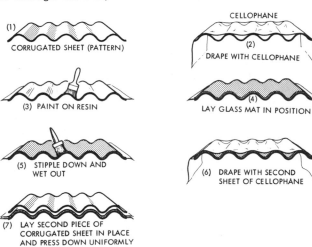

FIG. 15.3 MAKING CORRUGATED SHEET MOULDINGS

CHAPTER SIXTEEN

Tanks in GRP

GRP tanks for holding water or other liquids are invariably constructed with the smooth gel coat surface on the inside, i.e. they are laid up on a *male* mould. The exception to this is where an existing tank is being repaired or renovated by sheathing with GRP. In this case the sheathing should be applied to the *inside* of the tank is possible (e.g. if the lid is detachable, as on a water tank). Fluid pressure with a filled tank will then press the sheathing on to the original tank walls. If there is no access to the inside of the tank, sheathing or patch repairs will have to be made to the outside of the tank when the sheathing (or patch) will have to bear the full fluid pressure through any leak in the original tank.

For making a new GRP tank a CSM laminate is quite adequate. There is no need to use rovings or woven glasscloth, although where strength is critical a single layer of cloth may be used with CSM. Due consideration should be given to the choice of resin, however. All general purpose resins (and most others) still contain styrene when cured, although only in very small amounts (typically about 50 parts per million). Thus it is not harmful to humans, but in the case of a tank used to hold drinking water it will impart a 'taste' to the water which will persist for some time. This will be particularly noticed on GRP drinking water tanks for boats or caravans where the water is likely to remain unchanged for long periods at a time. It can

persist for many fillings of the tank. A new GRP tank for domestic water supplies, however, has its contents replaced regularly and the 'taste' of styrene will be washed out in a short time. In either case, however, use a resin approved for drinking water supplies (e.g. British Water Authority Approval).

Particular attention is necessary as regards the leaching out of styrene in GRP fishponds and garden pools. Styrene, even in minute amounts, is highly poisonous to fish and the finished pond needs to be styrene free before fish are introduced—see chapter 17.

With other types of tanks there should be few problems in choice of resin. Most general purpose resins are suitable for making fuel tanks, for example, although a chemically resistant resin is preferred for tanks holding diesel fuel. A chemically resistant resin should also be used for tanks holding chemically active fluids. In certain cases this may demand using epoxy or furane resin instead of polyester—see Appendix 4.

GRP Tank Design

The size of tank required is dictated by the *volume* required. Matching geometric proportions are easiest marked out for rectangular shapes. The final design of a rectangular tank, however, must incorporate generously rounded corners, not sharp edges. A normal allowance to ac-

MECHANICAL FASTENING WITH BONDING OR SEALER

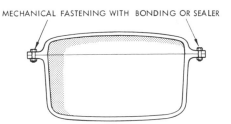

FIG. 16.1 DESIGN FOR A SEALED TANK

commodate the resulting loss of volume compared with a sharp-edge rectangle of similar overall dimensions is an extra 5% on purely rectangular volume. In other words, work on dimensions for a purely rect-angular tank accommodating 5% more than the required volume. It is, however, possible to construct purely rectangular tanks from flat sheet panels with suitable edge reinforcement.

Where relatively exact volumes are re-quired it is easiest to calculate in terms of a cylindrical tank, where no allowance is required for 'rounding' edges. In other applications the shape and/or size of the tank may be dictated by styling require-ments and/or the space available in which the tank has to be fitted.

To be constructed over a male mould the tank needs to be of two-part construction, each part being laid up over its own mould. Whenever possible the joint line should be positioned to come above the liquid level—i.e. the tank consisting of a deep tank section with a shallow lid—Fig. 16.1.

A flanged joint is to be preferred if the tank is to be sealed as this will give better control of the bonded joint, which can be clamped up during setting, or further se-cured, particularly if the tank is of stylised shape. Particular care must be taken over the bonding together of the two mould-ings if the joint line has to come below the normal level of the tank contents—e.g. see Fig. 16.2.

The possibility of using built-up con-struction, employing flat moulded sheets, should not be overlooked where a square, rectangular or wedgeshaped tank is re-quired. Joints can be reinforced with tape or mat or cloth strips—see Fig. 16.3. Whilst this eliminates the need for making special moulds, it does place a premium on ac-curate cutting to shape of the individual panels.

Fillers, mounting lugs, vent pipe fittings, brackets, etc., can readily be bonded in place with an overlay of glass mat.

In the case of tanks built to hold water or chemical solutions, the finished tank should be left to age for at least two to three weeks before being put into use in order to reach maximum resistance to water absorption and chemical attack.

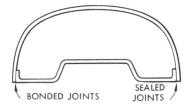

BONDED JOINTS   SEALED JOINTS

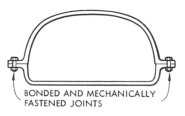

BONDED AND MECHANICALLY FASTENED JOINTS

FIG. 16.2

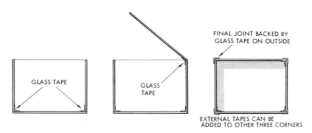

FINAL JOINT BACKED BY
GLASS TAPE ON OUTSIDE

GLASS TAPE

GLASS
TAPE

EXTERNAL TAPES CAN BE
ADDED TO OTHER THREE CORNERS

FIG. 16.3 RECTANGULAR TANKS FROM MOULDED SHEET PANELS

With petrol tanks an even longer ageing period is recommended, if possible. With petrol tanks, too, particular care should be taken during the lay-up to ensure a perfect gel coat of good thickness. Perfect sealing of the surface is important, as if stray glass fibres can become loosened they can be carried by the fuel into the carburettor and cause blockage. A slightly flexible resin for the gel coat might be an advantage to eliminate any possibility of the gel coat crazing or cracking under vibrational loads it might experience in service.

Treatment for Drinking Water Tanks

A minimum curing time for a drinking water tank is seven days in a warm atmosphere—longer if the temperature is cool. After that period *repeated* flushing out with *hot* water will remove most of the free styrene present. This needs to be done ten times at least to be properly effective. An even better method of removing the 'taste' of styrene is to flush repeatedly with steam—not something the amateur constructor can readily attempt, but there may be a local garage with facilities for steam cleaning who could do this job.

Repairing Old Tanks

Glass fibre is a very good medium for repairing leaky tanks of all kinds. The main requirement is that the tank is empty and quite dry. Loose corrosion and rust should be cleaned off the affected area with a wire

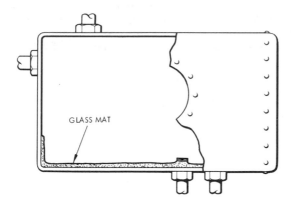

GLASS MAT

FIG. 16.4

95

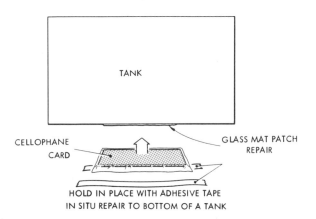

TANK

CELLOPHANE
CARD

GLASS MAT PATCH
REPAIR

HOLD IN PLACE WITH ADHESIVE TAPE
IN SITU REPAIR TO BOTTOM OF A TANK

FIG. 16.5

brush. The leak can then be repaired with a 'patch' of glass fibre mat, applied with resin.

In the case of a tank which can be opened the 'patch' repair is best applied on the inside, extending over as wide an area as necessary (Fig. 16.4). If perforation of the tank is very prominent, the outside surface should be backed up with a piece of cellophane covered card or hardboard, held in place with adhesive tape. The patch thickness can be quite generous—say three layers of $1\frac{1}{2}$ ounce mat for an average repair. The resin mix may have to be adjusted to suit the air temperature, if the tank is repaired *in situ*. Hardening off can be speeded by placing a suitable heater near the tank when the repair is completed. In the case of a repair to a cold water tank it is obvious that the tank is needed back in service as soon as possible. Use heat to post-cure and allow a minimum of twelve hours hardening time, if possible.

Sealed tanks, such as fuel tanks, must be patched on the outside, unless they have an inspection panel which can be removed and gives access to the damage from the inside. The procedure is essentially the same, but the tank must be fully emptied

and the patch area *completely degreased,* otherwise the resin will not adhere. This can be done by scrubbing with trichlorethylene, carbon tetrachloride, or a strong detergent solution. In the latter case, check that the damaged area is dried out thoroughly before proceeding with the repair. Even when dry on the outside, some moisture could remain inside the tank, where it has entered through the original damage.

If the repair has to be made *in situ* and is on the bottom of the tank (as is usually the case with a car petrol tank), the patch may have to be supported in place with a piece of cellophane covered card or hardboard, strapped to the bottom of the tank with adhesive tape (Fig. 16.5). The resin should have enough tackiness for the patch to be positioned properly, working from underneath. The additional back-up is to ensure that it does not sag or pull off under its own weight whilst setting.

Large metal storage tanks of welded construction may eventually fail at the seams. A replacement tank can be very expensive and so a repair job is usually worthwhile, even if all the seams of the tank are suspect as a consequence, or

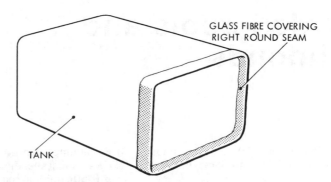

FIG. 16.6 REPAIRS TO A WELDED TANK

because of age. In this case the repair or overlay or glass fibre should be continued right round the complete length of seam, not confined to the damaged area (Fig. 16.6). In extreme cases it might even be considered advisable to clad the whole of the tank with glass fibre. In that case the original tank merely becomes an imperfect 'liner', but any further deterioration will not lead to a new leak developing. The liner will, however, be in direct contact with the contents and the corrosion products may be withdrawn with them. The chances of this happening can be minimised by flushing out the tank thoroughly with an inhibiting fluid.

CHAPTER SEVENTEEN

Garden pools and fishponds

The application of GRP to garden pools and fishponds falls into three different categories:

(i)   Repair of existing ponds which have developed leaks.

(ii) Sheathing (i.e. producing a waterproof inner liner) over a basic construction for a pond in brick or similar materials.

(iii) Construction of a complete glass fibre pool.

Repairs to existing ponds

Concrete ponds are prone to develop cracks which defy repair by further concrete or fillers. Glass fibre is potentially an excellent repair material, but the main difficulty lies in getting the damaged surface dry enough and clean enough for proper adhesion of a GRP patch or sheathing. If the damage is localised, a patch repair can prove quite satisfactory—until further cracks develop elsewhere. Overall sheathing is a longer-lasting proposition, but does require that the pond be pumped out completely, thoroughly cleaned out and allowed to dry. It can prove extremely difficult to achieve the latter in all but summer months. In fact, a more economic solution for a cracked pond is usually to fit it with a plastic sheet liner (e.g. polythene sheet pond lining).

If patch repairs or complete sheathing in GRP is attempted, however, the technique follows normal sheathing procedure using $1\frac{1}{2}$ oz ($450\,g/m^2$) or $2\,oz$ ($600\,g/m^2$) chopped strand mat and water-resistant resin (e.g. a resin formulated for marine work), over an initial layer of surfacing tissue. This layer will then act as a sealing layer to prevent a lot of resin being wasted by draining away into the concrete.

Sheathing New Pond Constructions

Attractive ponds and garden pools can be built up above ground level using brick, concrete blocks, etc. bonded with mortar, 'brickwork' fashion. No excavation work is involved, the actual surface of the ground forming the bottom of the pond. The whole interior surfaces are then sheathed with layers of chopped strand mat and resin, just like laying up a laminate in a female mould. The basic pond structure, in fact, forms the mould. The only difference is that the finished GRP laminate is permanently bonded to its 'mould' when finished.

In this case all the built up inner side surfaces are first sheathed with surfacing mat. The bottom, which is earth, can then be lined with several layers of stout brown paper. The idea behind this treatment is the same as before—to prevent resin waste through soakage away into the brickwork and ground when the chopped strand mat layers are laid up in place.

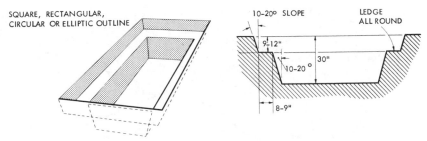

FIG. **17.1** FORMAL POOL PROPORTIONS

Sunken Pools

With a sunken pool, excavation takes the place of built-up construction, and again produces the necessary mould for the GRP laminate. The particular advantage offered by GRP here is that there is literally no restriction on the shape of the pool. It can be as curved or irregular as you like. However, there are certain basic design rules to follow:

(i) Regardless of the actual size, no pool needs to be deeper than 30 in. This will be sufficient to ensure that the pool will not freeze solid in winter, and also be deep enough to accommodate aquatic plants such as water lilies.

(ii) A minimum depth of 15-18 in is advisable, even for the smallest pools, in order to avoid excessive changes in water temperature between hot and cold weather.

(iii) Pond sides should slope outwards at an angle of about 20 degrees. This will eliminate the possibility of ice damage, and also ensure that the pool contains a reasonable volume of water for its surface area.

One other point can be considered before deciding on the pool proportions. Many aquatic plants, known as marginals, grow in fairly shallow water—preferring 3 to 5 in of soil with perhaps 6 to 9 in of water above. The design of a garden pool can therefore conveniently incorporate ledges around the edge on which marginal plants can be planted, or stood in pots. A ledge-shaped section will also be easier to excavate.

The basic requirements of a good pool design, therefore, work out as shown in Figs. 17.1 and 17.2. Fig. 17.1 is for a *formal* or geometric shape which may be rectangular, square, or even circular or elliptic. Fig. 17.2 is for an *informal* pool with an

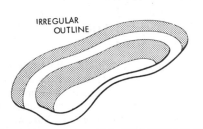

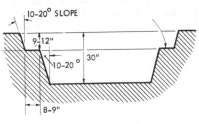

FIG. **17.2** INFORMAL POOL PROPORTIONS

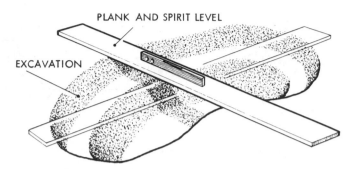

PLANK AND SPIRIT LEVEL

EXCAVATION

FIG. 17.3 CHECK EXCAVATION FOR LEVEL OF OUTLINE

irregular outline shape. Having decided on a shape, suitable size, and site, the next step is to dig out the ground to this shape. This is the hardest job of the lot.

It is important with a formal pool that the edges of the excavation should be level all round. If not the water level will lie at an angle to the edges of the pool and look wrong. This is less important in the case of an informal pool, but is again preferable. Check for level with a plank and a spirit level, laid across the excavation at various points (Fig. 17.3).

Preparation for the lay-up

The sides, shelves and bottom of the excavation need smoothing off as far as possible and at the same time should be pressed down to produce a well consolidated surface. Round off any sharp edges on shelves at the same time. Remove any stones which may appear at the surface and fill in any cavities produced with earth, pressed down in place.

You will now need enough sheets of good quality brown paper of the type with one shiny side to cover over the whole pool surface area with two or three layers, shiny side uppermost. Where necessary, hold the sheets of paper together with small pieces of cellulose tape. Flatten the paper lining down as far as possible and try to avoid getting too many wrinkles in it.

This preliminary lining is very necessary and serves two purposes. It will prevent the first application of resin soaking away into the earth and also prevent contact between resin and damp earth which would inhibit curing of the resin. It should also be obvious that the paper used should itself be quite dry, and the whole job of laying down the preliminary paper liner and the subsequent hand-lay-up of the resin and glass laminate over it be done in perfectly dry—and preferably warm—weather.

The one thing you do not want is for rain to wet the paper before you start the lay-up—or for it to rain before you have completed the laminate—so plan to do the whole operation in a single working session.

Laying up the Moulding

Laying up the moulding then follows normal GRP practice, except that you do not need a gel coat as such. The first coating, applied directly over the paper lining, should be of *air-inhibited resin,* applied in generous thickness. Allow ample time for this to gel, although the surface will remain tacky. Then follow normal hand-lay up procedure, stippling down each layer of chopped strand mat with a brush or roller-ing out, using a *low-styrene* laminating resin, not a general purpose resin.

The number of layers required will depend on the size of the pool. Two layers of $1\frac{1}{2}$ ounce ($450g/m^2$) mat should be adequate for most pools up to about 100 sq. ft (10 sq. metres) surface area, with additional layers for larger pools.

A final surfacing with glass fibre tissue is usually worthwhile, although this may be omitted on the grounds of expense. In any

case the finished moulding should be treated with a non-air inhibited 'gel' coat on the 'finished' side, followed by two or three coats of sealer or varnish to water-proof fully. The final gel coat can be coloured, if preferred.

The fact that the 'finished' or top surface of the GRP pool will appear rough is no disadvantage. In fact, it is more natural in appearance than the commercially pro-duced GRP pool liners which are almost invariably made on male moulds and thus have a smooth, shiny 'finished' surface.

The top edges of the pool should be trimmed off whilst still 'green', using tin-

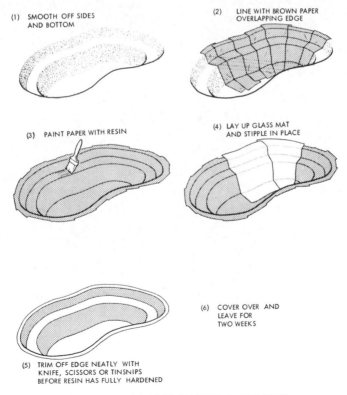

(1) SMOOTH OFF SIDES AND BOTTOM

(2) LINE WITH BROWN PAPER OVERLAPPING EDGE

(3) PAINT PAPER WITH RESIN

(4) LAY UP GLASS MAT AND STIPPLE IN PLACE

(5) TRIM OFF EDGE NEATLY WITH KNIFE, SCISSORS OR TINSNIPS BEFORE RESIN HAS FULLY HARDENED

(6) COVER OVER AND LEAVE FOR TWO WEEKS

FIG. 17.4 STAGES IN MAKING A GRP POOL

snips. Alternatively they can be flattened over the edge during moulding and subsequently covered with turf and/or flat stones.

Curing Time

The finished moulding should be left to cure for *at least* 14 days, preferably longer. During this time it should be covered over to prevent it getting damp if it rains. Even after it is fully cured it will still not be ready to fill and introduce fish because of the 'free' styrene content remaining. It needs filling, emptying and refilling several times over to reduce the final contamination of the water to absolute minimal levels. It is then better to introduce plants first, as they are less likely to be poisoned than fish, and if all seems well, introduce fish two or three weeks later. This will also help the plants establish themselves and promote properly balanced conditions for the fish.

CHAPTER EIGHTEEN

GRP in model making

To the model maker used to working mainly in woods, and to a lesser extent metals, moulded GRP constructions involve handling a much more 'messy' material, demanding new skills. However, GRP is a much more foolproof material in that shaping and finishing is controlled by a mould and laying up a laminate in a mould is a semi-skilled rather than a skilled job, so that one rapidly becomes familiar with the material and its characteristics. In other words, it is very easy to learn to use glass plastics properly, and extract full advantage from the material and the additional scope it brings.

Some particular modelmaking applications where GRP can produce superior results to conventional constructions are:— *Model Aircraft*—construction of moulded fuselages for radio controlled and control line models; construction of cowls for model engines; local reinforcement, etc. All can be tackled by hand lay-up. In addition glass-filled nylon mouldings are now commonly used to produce propellers with superior strength, and some model airscrews also incorporate carbon fibre reinforcement. Whilst these are normally commercial productions, the making of dies to use with a suitable technique (see chapter 2) is not beyond the skills of any reasonably competent model engineer. *Model Boats*—here the moulding of complete hulls is an obvious choice for GRP, the exceptional strength/weight ratio of

such a hull being especially valuable. No other modelling material is competitive on such a basis. Also, once a mould has been made, time to complete a hull moulding is but a fraction of that using traditional hull-building methods. Decks are another attractive subject for GRP, as these can be produced as one-piece mouldings complete with cabin and/or superstructure.

Model Aircraft Requirements

Model aircraft represent a rather special case in that although high strength is desirable, actual weight is the final criterion as far as free flight models go. Thus balsa wood is a standard structural material for model aircraft airframes. Nevertheless successful free flight models have been produced from glass plastic mouldings—with shell mouldings for the fuselage and wing and tail panels. In the main, however, these are restricted to radio control designs of generous size, where weight has a less critical effect on flight performance, and now almost entirely confined to moulded fuselage construction. These are produced in the form of half shell mouldings, suitably jointed. GRP mouldings would not normally be considered for wings or tail surfaces, owing to the difficulty of constructing such components, and the excess weight, compared with foam plastic construction.

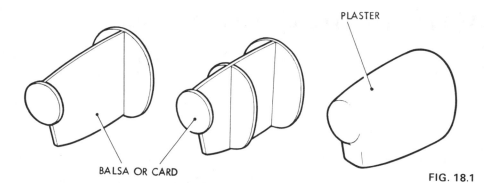

PLASTER

BALSA OR CARD

FIG. 18.1

The latter has adequate strength, at less weight, when skinned with thin balsa or hardwood veneer.

GRP is an excellent material for moulded cowlings. This part of a scale or semi-scale model is always difficult to produce. Close-fitting cowlings in balsa have to be hollowed out to a degree where they are inherently weak—and the cowling usually comes in for a lot of handling in starting the engine. Glass plastic is an excellent alternative, and a far more satisfactory material.

The cowling shape required is best built as a simple balsa sheet mock-up, as in Fig. 18.1, when it can be filled in with plasticine to complete a solid form. A glass plastic laminate can be laid directly over this, or a glass plastic female mould made first so that the outer surface of the final moulding is smooth. A single layer of 10-thou. cloth should provide adequate strength for small cowlings, but an additional layer of 1-ounce mat (or cloth again) is generally to be preferred. Lugs or suitable fittings for attachment can be mounted in the moulding whilst still wet, or bonded in later. Whether the cowling is designed to be detached and removed in one piece or split into two pieces depends on the model and motor mount it is to fit.

Spats, large fairings and similar relatively small, non-structural items can similarly be moulded in glass plastic. Another major use is for reinforcing the nose sections of large power models, particularly radio control models—see Fig. 18.2. A reinforcement of a single layer of thin glass cloth impregnated with resin is very much stronger than the conventional 'bandage and balsa cement' reinforcement. The

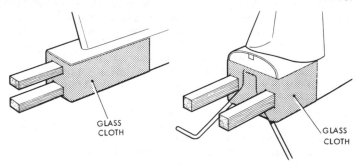

GLASS CLOTH

GLASS CLOTH

FIG. 18.2

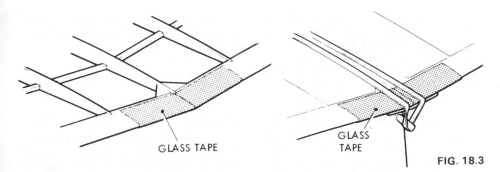

GLASS TAPE

GLASS TAPE

FIG. 18.3

same applies to local stress points on wing dihedral breaks and where wing attachments bands bear against the trailing edge (Fig. 18.3).

With control line models, weight is not so important and here the extra strength offered by glass plastics can be a considerable advantage. Stunt models are usually kept light, but with combat models (where toughness is essential), team racers and speed models there appears to be excellent scope for expanding the application of glass plastics—particularly as this field has so far been rather neglected.

The most logical application is to fuselages, moulded as half shells split either horizontally or vertically—see Fig. 18.4. A glass plastic pan can be made quite as strong as a light alloy 'speed pan' of the

same weight, whilst the upper shell can be kept quite thin and light as it is really only a fairing. The mould for the latter can be a simple mock-up in balsa and plasticine, and the time taken in producing a finished moulding probably no longer than doing a really first-class job in balsa construction. By making a female mould from the pattern and using pigmented resin, all the hard work associated with rubbing down and getting a good finish on a wood fuselage is avoided, and the problem of fuel proofing is overcome.

Similar considerations apply with team racer fuselages, although with a vertical split it will become necessary to incorporate internal bulkheads to carry the motor bearers. Once having produced a suitable mock-up fuselage and made a

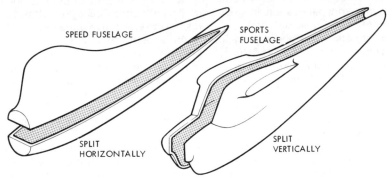

SPEED FUSELAGE

SPORTS FUSELAGE

SPLIT HORIZONTALLY

SPLIT VERTICALLY

FIG. 18.4

female mould from it, however, future production of team racer fuselages can proceed at a very high rate.

A glass plastic fuselage would probably best be associated with conventional wing and tail construction. Certainly there is no advantage in trying to make the tail surfaces from anything but balsa (or thin ply, if additional strength is required). The construction of wing 'envelopes' or half shells in glass plastic hardly appears worth the extra trouble involved, compared with carving from solid balsa or using conventional built-up construction. Nor would 'skinning' with thin glass cloth add greatly to the overall strength, the weakest point still being the bending strength at the roots where the wing joins the fuselage. Glass plastic sheathing would, however, protect leading edges against damage by 'notching'.

Model Boat Hulls

The beauty of GRP hulls is that they can readily be produced in any shape or size. Thus with conventional construction round bilge hulls are usually avoided for model power boat use, since they have to be carved and hollowed out, whilst the carving or planking of a racing yacht hull is a tedious, laborious process. Apart from the fact that you still have to construct a mould of some sort, fabrication in glass plastic is an easy and rapid solution.

For model boats up to about 10 in in length, a single layer of $1\frac{1}{2}$ (450g/m²) ounce may well provide more than adequate strength, but an additional layer may be considered advisable for rigidity. Two to three layers of $1\frac{1}{2}$ (450/gm²) ounce mat is adequate for hulls from 20 to 36 in in length. For still larger hulls—up to 60 in—three layers of $1\frac{1}{2}$ (450g/m²) ounce mat is recommended. Some modellers may prefer to use these recommended

weights of glass but employ 1 ounce (300g/m²) mat to increase the number of plies in the moulding.

Use a Female Mould

The method of working with a female mould can be used to duplicate existing hulls. Thus a standard plastic or wooden hull can become a master pattern or plug, once exterior fittings have been removed and the gunwale line built up to provide extra depth for trimming. The female mould can then be produced in GRP, laid-up over the original hull, or cast in plaster from this hull (Fig. 18.5). The latter is a quick and simple method of producing female moulds for one-off jobs.

So popular have GRP hulls become for model boats that a wide range of proprietary mouldings are now available, covering both power boat and yacht designs. Unless particularly committed to an original design, the individual builder will usually find these a better proposition than making his own mould and moulding as the saving in time and effort is usually well worth the extra cost which may be involved.

Subsequent treatment of a moulded glass plastic hull is very much a matter of personal choice and ingenuity. By leaving a 'lip' on the top of the moulding decks may be attached direct (Fig. 18.6) but this restricts the design to a straight deck line. It is more usual to trim the height of the mouldings to the deck line required, when the attachment of a wooden gunwale provides a fastening point for the deck beams as required, and the deck itself (Fig. 18.7).

Small glass plastic hulls—say up to 30 in length—will normally not require any internal frames or stiffening at all, sufficient rigidity being given by the deck. Bulkheads may be fitted for convenience, or to blank

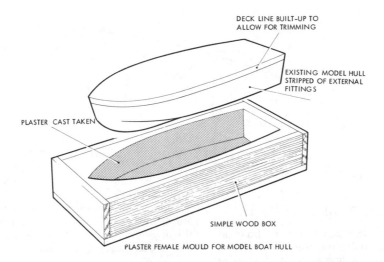

DECK LINE BUILT-UP TO
ALLOW FOR TRIMMING

EXISTING MODEL HULL
STRIPPED OF EXTERNAL
FITTINGS

PLASTER CAST TAKEN

SIMPLE WOOD BOX

PLASTER FEMALE MOULD FOR MODEL BOAT HULL

FIG. 18.5

off parts of the hull into watertight compartments. Equally, buoyancy compartments can be moulded in glass plastic and added to the moulding to give an 'unsinkable' hull. Frames and/or stiffeners will probably be required on larger hulls to ensure that the beam does not tend to spread, or even to control the final deck platform shape.

The absence—or near absence—of internal members, coupled with the thin skin required, means that a glass plastic hull is a very 'roomy' hull—with plenty of space for installing the power plant, radio control gear, etc., if required. Such fittings as are required, like motor bearers, etc., can be inserted whilst the laminate lay-up is still tacky, or bonded on with strips of resin-soaked glass cloth later. The builder has a very wide freedom of design choice in this respect. The two important things to bear in mind are that the finished hull will only be as true as the original pattern and its strength and durability will depend on following the correct lay-up technique, eliminating air bubbles and ensuring adequate impregnation of the glass fibre reinforcement with the resin. Grade 'E' cloth or mat should always be used for hull construction.

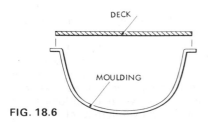

DECK

MOULDING

FIG. 18.6

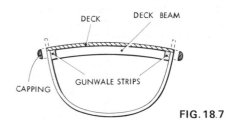

DECK   DECK BEAM

CAPPING

GUNWALE STRIPS

FIG. 18.7

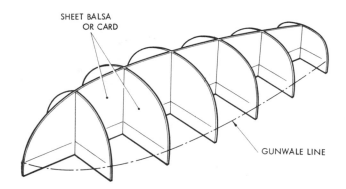

SHEET BALSA
OR CARD

GUNWALE LINE

FIG. 18.8

Making a Plug

A plug for a hull can readily be built up from card or balsa patterns taken off the hull plan—assembling in skeleton form as in Fig. 18.8. The pattern can be completed by filling in between the bulkhead patterns with scrap material to bulk, and finally completing the shape with plaster or plasticine. If smoothed right off (and in the case of the plaster mould, coated with shellac and waxed) this can be used to produce a *male* mould over which a GRP laminate is laid up to produce a *female* mould in which the final hull moulding is laid up.

This may appear a duplication of effort, but the result is certainly worthwhile and the additional time spent not very great. The GRP female mould, too, is available for further use, it required, whereas the original male mould may have to be broken down to withdraw the first moulding, if the shape includes any undercuts. Undercuts would be accommodated on a female mould by making this mould in two halves, to be bolted together as in Fig. 18.9.

An alternative method which can be used for making a hull which has marked undercutting or tumblehome is to eliminate the transom from the moulding. In other words, the stern end of the mould is left open. The moulding can then be sprung out of the mould without much difficulty and a separate transom then fitted to complete the hull—see Fig. 18.10.

Superstructure

Other marine model items which can be tackled in glass plastic include complete superstructures with internal decks, deck cabins, etc., and even smaller fittings like dinghies, hatches, engine-box covers and so on. There is certainly no need to stop short at hulls when thinking in terms of glass plastic construction for marine models. You have at your call a material as strong as steel, easily formed to almost any shape (although very small mouldings are tricky to handle), and one which is light and permanent. Nor can the possibility of using resin castings be overlooked.

The strength of a GRP hull is, proportionately, very much higher than a full-size moulded glass-plastic hull, with the weight still comparable—and probably less—than a built up or carved wooden hull. It can be expected to take almost any knocks the craft is likely to receive in service without damage. Using a pigment in the resin coats, the hull can be self-coloured and will continue to look smart and 'new' for years. Alternatively, existing

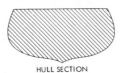

HULL SECTION

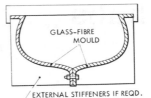

GLASS–FIBRE
MOULD

/ EXTERNAL STIFFENERS IF REQD.

FIG. 18.9

wooden hulls can be sheathed in glass plastic to give watertightness and added strength, as in the case of full size boat hulls—see chapter 21. In such cases a single layer of 1 ounce mat should be adequate for the job on any size of hull, or even a single layer of surfacing tissue.

Model Cars

For duplicating model car bodies rapidly for use on rail-track conversions, etc., a standard plastic car body can be a 'ready made' pattern for making a female mould in glass plastic. From this mould any number of duplicates can be made with a minimum of trouble—in a variety of colours if you wish. Freelance car body designs can be tackled on basic lines, starting with the construction of a full size plug, on the same lines as for a full size car body described in chapter 22.

Model Railway Layouts

Model railway layouts can benefit greatly from the scenic effects such as hills, cuttings, tunnels and 'landscape' forms, readily produced in glass cloth impregnated with resin and laid over chicken wire, balled-up newspaper, etc., to arrive at the required contours. This is probably the easiest method of tackling such layouts—very much quicker and simpler than using papier-mache, and more durable than hessian soaked in plaster.

The scope of glass plastic modelling can also be extended to architectural models, display layouts of all kinds and all other spheres where fabricated models are normally employed. Where certain items are duplicated (e.g. types of buildings), preparation of a single mould enables the complete number required to be turned out with the minimum of time and trouble.

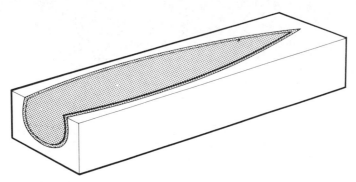

FIG. **18.10** OPEN-ENDED MOULD—Enabling moulding to be 'sprung' out

CHAPTER NINETEEN

GRP hulls

Boat construction is probably the biggest single application of GRP. Unfortunately, it is also the least suited to amateur construction, primarily because hull moulding virtually demands the use of a female mould. This means the construction of a full size plug first, on which the mould is laid up (invariably in GRP). The method is both lengthy, and expensive, for one-off productions.

It is, however, possible to construct a female mould direct, provided the builder is reasonably skilled as a carpenter and can interpret hull line drawings. Thus the job should be within the scope of any modeller or handyman to attempt the construction of a full size dinghy or runabout in GRP.

The simplest hull form to attempt is the deep-vee powerboat hull form with con-stant deadrise, this being originally de-signed to be constructed from flat ply panels, and thus free from compound curves. It is possible to reproduce such a hull form from five flat panels of hardboard, suitably assembled and braced in an external framework, as shown in Fig. 19.1.

Hull lines can be taken off any suitable scale drawing of a full size hull. The external frames should be erected first, made from any suitable wood, screwed rigidly together. The skin panels are then attached to these frames, using a minimum number of countersunk head screws, with the head pulled down below the surface of the hardboard. Bottom panels can be finally fitted up by cut-and-try methods. Gaps or bad fits are not necessarily important as these can be filled in as

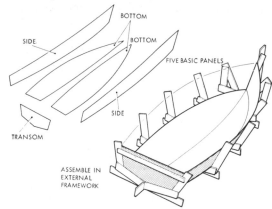

FIG. 19.1 CONSTRUCTION OF A FEMALE HULL MOULD

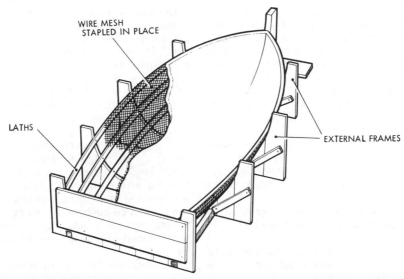

WIRE MESH
STAPLED IN PLACE

LATHS

EXTERNAL FRAMES

FIG. 19.2 LATH AND PLASTER FEMALE MOULD CONSTRUCTION

necessary. The main object is to complete a 'hollow' hull shape with the surface of the mould completely uncluttered so that it can be made good as necessary, smoothed right off and polished in the manner of a female mould. Small deviations in shape from the original drawings could be quite acceptable, provided the hull form produced remained perfectly symmetrical.

No attempt should be made to 'cut in' chines and longitudinal strakes on the bottom (essential for stability of a deep-vee hull). This would only make the mould construction unnecessarily tedious, as well as making lay-up in the finished mould more difficult. Such items can be mounted later on the finished moulding.

Various refinements are possible on this relatively straightforward method of female construction. Thus the deadrise or vee-angle could be greatly reduced, and the sharp angle between bottom panels and sides could be rounded off with a fillet of plaster, producing more of a round bilge

form, suitable for a sailing dinghy or utility runabout rather than a speedboat.

True round bilge forms are more difficult to mock up since this would normally call for several external, and accurately plotted, frames on which are fastened laths bent to the right curvature. These laths would need close spacing, especially in regions of double curvature, and tapering off at the bows and stern where they would tend to become crowded together (Fig. 19.2).

Such a mock-up could be completed, as a mould, by covering with wire mesh, held in place with small staples, followed by draping in hessian soaked in plaster. Once this had hardened in position, a rough coating of plaster trowelled on and smoothed out, followed by a smooth final plaster coating completes the mould to a stage where it is ready for final smoothing, sanding down and sealing.

Moulds of this type may take less time to make than a plug, from which a female mould is to be taken in GRP. A plug, however, has the advantage that it is 'the right way round' rather than a three-dimensional 'image' of the actual hull, and thus it is easier to appreciate the shapes involved, where they may need modification, and so on. The other two advantages of a plug are:

(i)   Compound curves can more readily be incorporated, particularly to improve bow shapes.

(ii)   Appendages such as chines, keel, external strakes, etc., can readily be added to the plug, and thus incorporated in the GRP mould when made.

Fig. 19.3 shows a suitable method of making a plug for a round bilge hull.

A plug for a hard chine hull could be made directly from flat panels assembled on a simple internal framework.

Construction of a plug for a female mould can be eliminated if a suitable subject can be found ready-made. For example, an existing hull of suitable size and a shape can be used directly as a plug. The only work involved then is stripping off appendages and fittings which would interfere with the production of a suitable GRP mould, when laid up on it, and making good, sealing and finishing the surface of the hull to a suitable standard for taking a moulding off. This can be the major work involved in such a project. Starting with an old hull, though, which will not be used again, various modifications can be built on to the original hull to improve the shape, again using the simplest and cheapest materials available for the job.

A further possibility worth investigating is the *hire* of female moulds for GRP hull

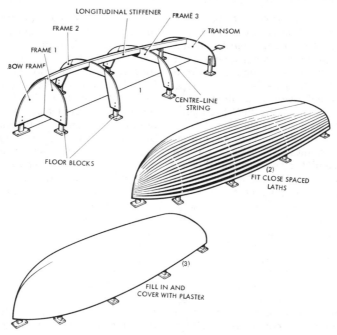

FIG. 19.3

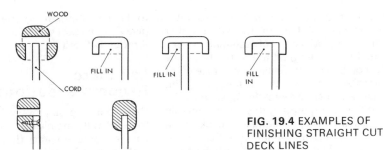

FIG. 19.4 EXAMPLES OF
FINISHING STRAIGHT CUT
DECK LINES

construction. These are available in various sizes and designs, covering canoes up to small yachts and motor boats.

Moulds for hull designs must allow for trimming of the final moulding, and how the top line of the hull is to be finished. Fig. 19.4 shows various methods of finishing off a plain trimmed hull moulding, such as might be used in small open boats. The incorporation of a 'rolled over' edge in such cases is good practice, adding considerable stiffness and rigidity to the top lines of the hull. Such 'rolled-over' sections should always be filled.

Where the hull is to be fitted with a deck, then a flanged edge is preferable so that

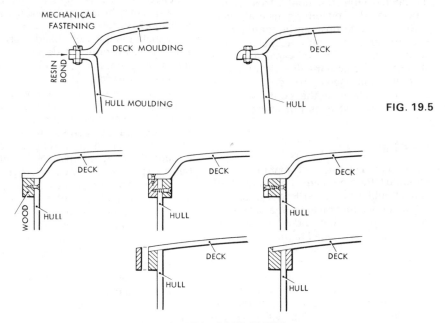

FIG. 19.5

FIG. 19.6 HULL–DECK JOINTS

the hull and deck moulding can be screwed, stapled, bolted or riveted together (Fig. 19.5). Mechanical fastening is preferred to bonding, although the two may be combined (or sealer used instead of adhesive) to ensure a watertight joint. There are alternative methods, such as the addition of separate gunwale and inwale pieces to provide a seating for a deck, and a number of possible variations are shown in Fig. 19.6. This by no means exhausts the possibilities.

Interior Frames

Interior frames, etc., are normally constructed of solid mahogany, or sometimes ply, and bonded in place with strips of glass mat, as shown in Fig. 19.7. These are fitted after the moulding has set, but before it is removed from the mould. There is then little or no risk of disturbing the hull shape.

Stiffeners and ribs can be moulded in-situ around any suitable core material—e.g. wood, strips of foam or paper rope. The strength of the core material is not important. It merely serves to form the GRP section in place. If the core itself later deteriorates, that does not matter.

Decks

Decks can be made of marine ply, or separate GRP mouldings. Logically a GRP hull should have a GRP deck, but for amateur construction at least a ply deck is much simpler to cut and fit. A separate female mould is needed to produce a GRP deck moulding. The same applies where the boat is to have a cabin as well. Ply and solid mahogany construction will provide the quickest, simplest and cheapest answer for a one-off job. If a GRP moulding is considered, however, this will have the advantage that deck and cabin sides and

roof can be moulded in one piece and will give a permanent structure free from leaks, if properly fitted.

Laminate Recommendations

Glass mat is to be preferred to glass cloth for GRP hulls, mainly because it is easier to ensure complete and thorough wetting with resin using this material. Hulls laminated from cloth have, in the past, often suffered from de-lamination, where the first or outside layer starts to peel off, particularly if the workmanship was not up to suitable standards in the first place.

Glass mat can therefore be taken as suitable for all types and sizes of boat hulls, provided it is used in suitable weight or total thickness. If additional strength is required for any particular reason, then glass mat may be interposed with a layer of woven rovings.

Actual thicknesses used vary considerably with different designers. Those intent on economy of materials will use minimum thicknesses. Thus one finds recommendations of two layers of $1\frac{1}{2}$ ounce ($450\,g/m^2$) mat as suitable for hulls up to 10ft (3m) long or more. In practice this must be considered inadequate as although such a hull may be strong enough it will inherently lack rigidity and be very springy. Also, apart from reducing cost, there is nothing to be gained by using a minimum thickness of hull moulding. GRP construction is very light, and GRP hulls are often so light as to need additional ballast. It is more realistic to incorporate more bulk and weight of GRP in the actual hull.

The following recommendations are given as a general guide, based on the use of glass fibre mat reinforcement through-out:

Hulls up to 10ft (3 metres)—$4\frac{1}{2}$ ounces of

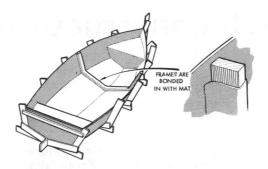

FRAMES ARE
BONDED
IN WITH MAT

FIG. 19.7

glass per square foot (1350g/m²), e.g. three layers of 1½ ounce (450g/m²) chopped strand mat.

Hulls 10-14ft (3-4.5 metres)—6 ounces of glass per square foot (1.8kg/m²), e.g. four layers of 1½ ounce (450g/m²) CSM; or three layers of 2oz (600g/m²) CSM.

Hulls 15-18ft (4.5-6 metres)—7½ ounces of glass per square foot (2.25kg/m²), e.g. five layers of 1½oz (450g/m²) CSM.

Hulls 18-24ft (5.5-7.5 metres)—9 to 12 ounces of glass per square foot (2.7-3.6kg/m²), with a minimum of *five* layers.

For further guidance—and especially in the case of larger hulls—consult the Boat Reports in the yachting journals. These usually quote glass weight used and may also include typical sections showing where extra reinforcement is used.

On certain designs, notably fast run-abouts and speedboats, and keel boats, thickness will need increasing locally with additional layers of mat. Thus an 18ft speedboat, for example, may have a hull based on 5 layers of 1½ ounce (450g/m²) mat, but with up to possibly 15 layers in highly stressed points, such as around the chines. The transom, too, will need additional stiffening, especially if it is to take an outboard motor or an inboard-outboard unit. Virtually standard practice here is to use sandwich construction for the transom, with the core of marine ply ranging in thickness from ¾in (19mm) upwards.

Where weight saving is important, as in the case of a racing yacht, thickness may vary from a maximum at the keel to a minimum over the topsides. For example, as little as 3 ounces per sq ft (900g/m²) may be considered adequate weight for the hull above the waterline, increasing to 4½ ounces per sq ft (1.2kg/m²) in the deck areas, and below the waterline. In the case of a keel yacht this would be further increased in the region of the keel, depending on the keel weight.

For readers wishing to study this subject in more detail, a copy of Lloyd's recommendations for GRP hull construction will provide a useful reference. It should be pointed out, however, that most professional builders work to their own specific ideas, and usually in excess of Lloyd's requirements.

The lay-up of glass fibre hulls follows the same technique described in chapter 11. The glass reinforcement used should be of 'E' grade. Surfacing tissue or surfacing mat is recommended for use both immediately following the gel coat, and as a final layer on the lay-up, although the latter is not invariably employed. Thixotropic resins are recommended throughout to eliminate draining. Any colouring or fillers used should be restricted to the gel coat.

CHAPTER TWENTY

Sandwich construction

The incorporation of ribs or stiffeners to reduce the deflection of GRP panels under load has already been described in chapter 9. An alternative method of providing stiffness is with a *sandwich laminate* consisting of two facing layers of GRP applied to a low density core material—Fig. 20.1. The resulting increase in stiffness can be quite remarkable since the stiffness or rigidity of a flat panel is proportional to the *cube* of its thickness. A sandwich moulding, using a lightweight core material, gives extra thickness without adding too much weight. In fact it can be both much stiffer, much lighter *and* cost less because the amount of GRP required is reduced.

As an example, take a select GRP moulding $\frac{3}{16}$in thick (5mm thick) and compare it with a sandwich of two $\frac{1}{16}$in GRP skins over a $\frac{1}{4}$in core (Fig. 20.2). This is twice as thick as the solid GRP panel, so the stiffness of this mould would be *8 times as rigid*. There is also a 33% saving in the amount of glass and resin used, and the panel would also be lighter.

Taking the comparison further by reducing the GRP skins to $\frac{1}{32}$in thick on a $\frac{1}{8}$in core, the total thickness is now the same,

so the stiffness would be the same as the solid GRP panel. But the amount of glass and resin is now reduced to one third of the original amount—a saving of $66\frac{2}{3}$ per cent. Using this same skin thickness again and increasing the core thickness to $\frac{5}{16}$in would again result in a panel eight times as stiff as the solid GRP. In both cases there would be substantial savings in weight as well as cost.

The limiting factor in sandwich construction is the minimum thickness required in the two GRP skins. Under beinding load the upper skin is in compression and the lower skin in tension—Fig. 20.3. Since GRP is normally stronger in tension than compression, this would imply using a greater thickness for the upper skin, which would also be useful in giving this skin better impact resistance. Commonly, however, the same thickness of GRP skin is used on each side of the core. The upper skin (subject to compressive loading) is then made adequately thick. The lower skin is then stronger than it need be, but this is not necessarily a bad thing.

If you actually know what flexural rigidity you need, the chart (Fig. 20.4) will

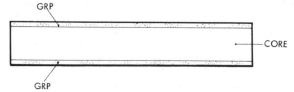

GRP

CORE

GRP

FIG. 20.1

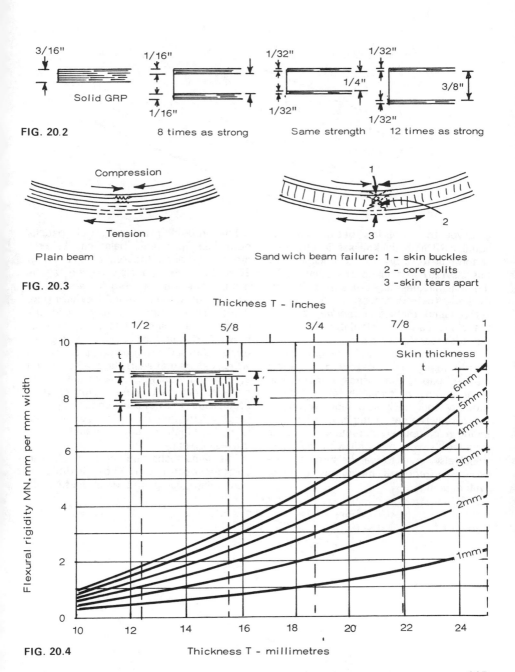

FIG. 20.2   8 times as strong   Same strength   12 times as strong

Plain beam

Sandwich beam failure: 1 - skin buckles
2 - core splits
3 - skin tears apart

FIG. 20.3

FIG. 20.4

117

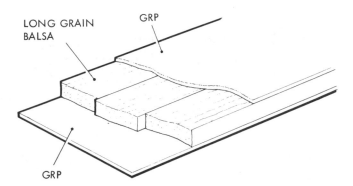

LONG GRAIN BALSA

GRP

GRP

give you the necessary design data for equal GRP skin thicknesses in chopped strand mat for a given *total* thickness. In this case the *core* thickness required will be the total thickness less twice the GRP skin thickness (core thickness=T−2t).

If required, the actual *bending stress* in the skins can be calculated from the formulae (see Appendix 9).

Suitable core materials include balsa, plastic foam, or honeycomb materials made of paper, composites or metal. The latter group are generally excluded for ordinary work, because of high cost. Balsa is probably the best material where a high strength, completely durable sandwich is required. It wets out well with the resin, which also serves to seal the surface of the wood and render it impervious to rot or waterlogging.

For producing flat sandwich panels, normal straight grain balsa can be employed, laid out in the form of sheets (Fig. 20.5). For curved panels end grain balsa is used, consisting of blocks about 2 in square, cut to the required thickness (Fig. 20.6). These blocks can be laid individually to match almost any type of curve. End grain blocks can also be glued up to a thin scrim to form complete panels which can be draped in place, when laying up in GRP moulding. In this case the scrim material may be terylene, nylon or glass fibre tissue. The adhesive commonly used for gluing the individual blocks to the scrim is PVA, which is fully compatible with polyester resin.

The same technique can be applied to amateur constructions. The main difficulty here when using end grain balsa is to

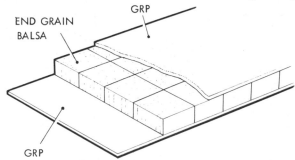

END GRAIN BALSA

GRP

GRP

ensure that the blocks are cut to exactly the same thickness throughout the finished moulding. Individual blocks should be cut on a sawbench, or in a jig. Hand sawing, or attempting to face individual blocks down to the same thickness, is not practical.

The particular virtue of end grain balsa is its high compressive strength. The use of end grain balsa as a core material, therefore, not only increases the stiffness of the GRP moulding but also its compressive strength and resistance to impact.

The added strength is directly related to the density of balsa used, which also affects the total weight of the laminate. Light density balsa should be selected for lightweight sandwich construction, as stiffness is largely independent of the core strength.

For the very lightest sandwich constructions, plastic foam is normally used for the core. All the foam materials have certain limitations as regards suitability and durability, however. Many tend to crumble or fail in use, with resulting loss of mechanical performance from the sandwich because of the break-up of the core.

Only polyurethane foam and *unplasticised* rigid PVC foam can be used as core materials without pretreatment. Phenolic foam needs pretreatment with a thixotropic resin mixture before using to seal the surface and prevent penetration of lay-up resin into the foam. Whilst penetration is not necessarily harmful, it increases the weight of the sandwich, and also the cost, because of the greater quantity of resin absorbed.

Plasticised PVC foam needs sealing before use as a core material as otherwise the resin may attack and soften the foam. Expanded polystyrene is rapidly attacked by the resin, but can be used if the surface is first fully sealed. Expanded rubber foam also needs to be sealed with shellac, or a special primer. Plastic foam materials which form a skin, either naturally, or after sealing, may also need their surface roughened before laying-up in order to ensure proper adhesion to the resin. Balsa, as a core material, is free from such limitations.

For calculations on strength and rigidity requirements, see also Appendix 9.

CHAPTER TWENTY-ONE

Sheathing hulls

Glass fibre may be used to sheath new wooden hulls to provide surface protection (e.g. against worm attack in warmer waters) or to renovate old hulls. In the former case only a very thin layer of glass is required, normally a single layer of lightweight cloth or in some cases surfacing tissue, laid on with laminating resin. Some authorities recommend sheathing only up to the waterline since this provides surface protection and watertightness where it is most required, and still permits a normal high gloss finish on the more visible (wooden) hull surface. In practice this is not to be recommended as the integrity of the sheathing treatment can be suspect around the top edge of the reinforcement. In fact, where sheathing of new wooden hulls is contemplated, nylon is the more usual choice for sheathing material, applied with a suitable adhesive (e.g. resorcinol resin). Even this practice has largely been discontinued.

The most practical application of GRP to sheathing hulls is in renovating old wooden hulls which have deteriorated badly, or have even developed rot. The amount of labour time to do this properly is considerable—and material costs can also run high. 'Carpentry' repairs can be simpler and cheaper in many cases, but demand considerable more skill and will not be as long lasting as properly done GRP renovation.

Glass fibre sheathing as a means of renovating an old wooden hull has many apparent attractions. Two or three layers of mat will build up a skin of sufficient thickness to provide complete strength, yet at the same time retain sufficient flexibility for the hull to 'work', if necessary (this applying more to planked hulls than ply skinned hulls). It will also give the wood a permanent waterproof coating.

In practice, these advantages can be largely offset by the enormous amount of time and effort which may be needed to bring the original hull into a suitable state *for* sheathing. Also unless the work can be carried out in dry conditions, no attempt at sheathing will be successful. The original hull wood must be *thoroughly dry* throughout, which may take several months even under favourable indoor storage.

Drying out of an old clinker or carvel built hull will also result in shrinkage, although this need not present a major problem. In the case of carvel construction, all loose caulking should be removed (clinker hulls are not caulked), and made good by filling flush with the surface with resin/filler or polyester filler. Original defects made good with putty or marine stopper must be gouged out and refilled with resin/filler.

Sheathing is *always* done on the outside surfaces of the hull—never the inside, or both sides. It will be virtually impossible to gain complete access to the inside for cleaning, etc. in any case. Sheathing both sides of a wooden hull would simply encourage the wood to rot.

Preparation of Hull Surface

Before any of this can be started, however, the whole hull surface must be stripped right down to bare wood. Paint is best removed with a paint stripper rather than burning off, as charred wood will not provide a satisfactory bond for the resin and may inhibit setting in such areas. Equally all paint and all oil-bound fillers must be removed.

It will also be necessary to remove any grease or oil which may have been absorbed by the wood. Swabbing the affected area with carbon tetrachloride or strong detergent solution is probably most effective here, but again may take considerable time to get all the oil out of the wood. Naturally oily wood, like genuine teak, may not be suitable for sheathing at all. It largely depends on how 'dry' it has become over the years.

All traces of rot or damage must also be cut out and repaired with new wood, or polyester filler. In the case of a clinker built hull it will also be advisable to fair in the bottom of each plank with lengths of triangular section wood, as shown in Fig. 21.1, or round these edges off generously to eliminate the sharp edges which would otherwise be difficult to cover round satisfactorily with the sheathing. These wood strips should be glued in place, using conventional resins, and also nailed at intervals to hold in place until set. Only copper nails should be used for this purpose, which will require the drilling of a hole to take each nail.

The success of a sheathing job will be as good as the preparation of the outer hull surface to a smooth, clean, paint and grease-free condition—and whether the wood is really dry or not when the actual sheathing is done. The sheathing part is usually the least laborious part of the whole job, but it will be the most expensive, for a considerable quantity of glass mat and resin may be involved.

Sheathing Materials

For a hull which is reasonably sound and does not require sealing of major leaks, a single layer of $1\frac{1}{2}$ ounce ($450g/m^2$) or 2 ounce ($600g/m^2$) mat may be adequate applied over a gel coat and finished off with a second gel coat or surface tissue. For hulls in poor condition two or three layers of $1\frac{1}{2}$ ounce ($450g/m^2$) may be needed. Thixotropic resins should be used throughout.

First step in sheathing is to paint the prepared hull surface all over with a generous coating of well catalysed laminating resin (preferably part air-

FIG. 21.1

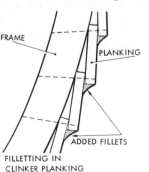

FRAME

PLANKING

ADDED FILLETS

FILLETTING IN
CLINKER PLANKING

inhibited type). This will not only help provide a good keying surface but will also show up soft parts which soak up the resin (these will look dull rather than glossy). These areas will need a further coat or two of resin. Use *laminating resin* for this pre-coat treatment, not so-called sheathing primer which is more often than not an accelerator rather than a resin.

Fillers should not be used in the resin. Pigments may be added for colouring, although again plain resin is probably best, using an overall paint finish for colouring.

To obtain as good a surface finish as possible the final layer can be of surfacing tissue, allowed to harden, and then followed by a final coat of laminating resin forming in effect a gel coat (but do not use a *gel coat* resin for this). This final resin coat could well be pigmented.

To finish for *painting*, the sheathing needs to be rubbed down with very fine abrasive to get the whole surface as flat and matt as possible. The best finishing paint to use is then two-part epoxy in the colour required, applied as two coats. The second coat is applied as soon as the first coat has hardened sufficiently to take it. If the first coat is allowed to harden fully, the second epoxy paint coating may lack adhesion and eventually peel off.

To be even more correct, if you are prepared to go to the trouble, epoxy is the best type of paint to use on *underwater* surfaces and polyurethane the best paint for above-water surfaces exposed to sunlight. This same dual-paint system applies equally well to painting glass fibre hulls.

Deck Sheathing

Glass fibre scrim or open 'string weave' applied directly to wooden decks with polyester resin provides a durable, waterproof covering far superior to canvas. The resin used can be pigmented to give a suitably coloured deck. Using a single layer of reinforcement the scrim pattern will be duplicated in the surface, if the resin coating is not too generous, which will impart a proportion of 'non-slip' properties. This can be improved by dusting the resin with fine sand, whilst still wet and tacky, and smoothing out uniformly. Loose sand can then be brushed off when the resin has set.

Similar considerations apply as for sheathing. The deck must be stripped completely of old paint, etc., and cleaned right down to bare wood to ensure proper adhesion of the resin. If the deck has previously been covered with a rubber sheeting material, a solvent should be used to remove any remaining traces of adhesive. Above all, the deck surface must be dry before attempting to apply the resin and scrim.

CHAPTER TWENTY-TWO

GRP car bodies

Construction of a GRP car body from scratch has a particular appeal to the 'special' builder since he can develop his own original ideas on form and shape. A considerable amount of work is involved before the actual car body can be moulded, however, and involves the following basic stages.

Design

The critical dimensions involved in design are summarised in Fig. 22.1. This basic layout should be drawn up, to a suitably large scale—not smaller than one-tenth full size, and preferably larger.

The *wheelbase dimension* largely de-termines the disposition of the 'working' components—engine and gearbox, pro-peller shaft and differential—and the *ground clearance* the lower level limit for the engine sump and body floor, bearing in mind that appendages such as the silencer must be taken into account. The *wheel* sizes can then be drawn into scale to give the required position and clearances for the wheel arches (Fig. 22.2).

Provision now has to be made to accommodate the driver and passenger(s) in the overall design. A scale human figure, with correct joint pivot positions, is shown in Fig. 22.3. These proportions are typical for a 5 ft 10 in man. They can be adjusted to other heights, if necessary, bearing in mind

FIG. 22.1

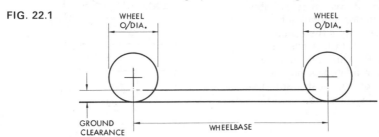

WHEEL O/DIA.

WHEEL O/DIA.

GROUND CLEARANCE

WHEELBASE

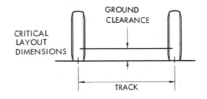

CRITICAL LAYOUT DIMENSIONS

GROUND CLEARANCE

TRACK

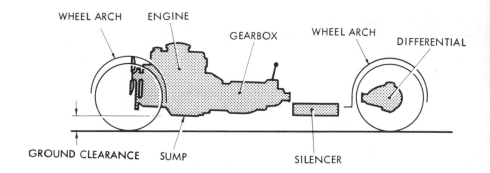

WHEEL ARCH   ENGINE   GEARBOX   WHEEL ARCH   DIFFERENTIAL

GROUND CLEARANCE   SUMP   SILENCER

that difference in height in human figures is *usually produced by differences in leg length only,* not overall scaling up or down.

A simple pattern of this figure can be constructed in thick card, with joints pivoted with paper fasteners, to the correct scale. This can be positioned over the drawing to determine seat position and driving attitude, and also the best control positions. Once the figure has been adjusted to a suitable position, it can be drawn round (Fig. 12.4). The side view body shape can then be drawn in to suitably envelope all the 'contents' involved.

An end view drawing is then prepared. The critical dimension in this case is the track (Fig. 22.5). Bear in mind the body width to be accommodated, which determines the width of the seats, and the necessary clearances across the section.

Scale Model

A scale model should then be made from these drawings. This can be a relatively simple mock-up, based on wood blocks, etc., finished off with plasticine or modelling clay, or carved to shape. The former is the more flexible method, for it enables detail changes to be made very easily, and is also much quicker.

The Plug

A full size mock-up or plug must be constructed next, scaled up from the model. Again slight changes can be introduced, if thought necessary. Equally, the

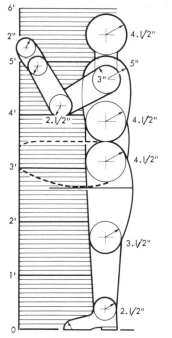

FIG. 22.3 HUMAN FIGURE PROPORTIONS

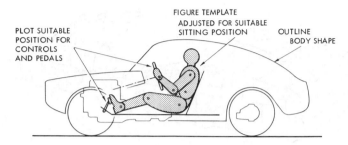

FIG. 22.4 POSITIONING THE DRIVER

scale model stage can be omitted entirely, relying on introducing necessary changes from the original drawing in the full size mock-up stage. However, a scale model does give a 'preview' of the mock up, and is a worthwhile extra stage. Much depends also on whether the builder is more competent as a draughtsman or modeller. In the former case he will probably get better results by going direct from drawing to mock-up stage. In the latter case, the drawing will give necessary proportions only, and virtually all the styling and shaping will be done 'by eye' through the model and mock-up stages.

The mock-up construction follows the same principles as that for making up any large mould—the simplest method usually being that of making a basic frame which can be draped with wire mesh, followed by hessian and plaster. Alternatively an 'egg-box' construction can be used, to be draped and covered with plaster—e.g. Fig. 22.6.

The Female Mould

Whilst a moulding can be taken directly off the mock-up, this will have a rough outer surface. In view of the amount of work already done by this stage, therefore, it is far better to lay up a female mould in GRP over the mock-up from which the final body moulding is taken. Although this

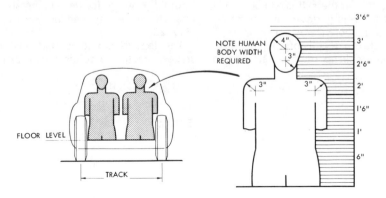

FIG. 22.5 FINALISING THE MAIN CROSS-SECTION

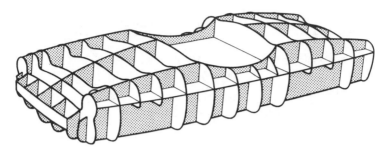

FIG. 22.6 EGG BOX CONSTRUCTION FOR BODY PATTERN

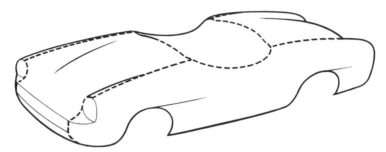

FIG. 22.7 EDGE TRIMMING LINES AND SEPARATION LINES FOR BONNET

involves additional time and expense, the finished result will more than justify this difference. There is also one positive saving in that the moulding taken off a female mould can be self coloured, eliminating the rubbing down and painting which would otherwise be necessary with a moulding taken directly off the mock-up.

First the mock-up must be studied to decide how many separate parts are required in the final body shape. These should be reduced to a minimum, e.g. separate bonnet and possibly separate boot lid. Having decided on suitable joint lines, these are marked on the mock-up (Fig. 22.7).

The female mould is then laid up in stages, erecting a suitable dam or barrier

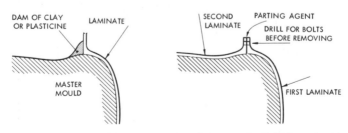

FIG. 22.8 INCORPORATION FLANGES ON SEPARATE MOULDINGS

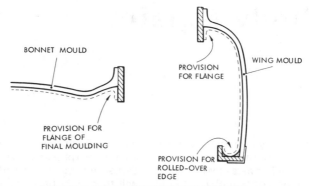

BONNET MOULD

PROVISION
FOR FLANGE

WING MOULD

PROVISION FOR
FLANGE OF
FINAL MOULDING

PROVISION FOR
ROLLED-OVER
EDGE

FIG. 22.9 MODIFICATIONS TO MOULDS

along the joint line(s). This can be built up with plasticine, as shown in Fig. 22.8. The first laminate is then laid up to this line, carried up the edge of the dam to form a flange. When set, the original dam can be removed and the flange on the first moulding can act as a dam for the second moulding, suitably protected with parting agent. The female mould is thus built up in separate sections. Necessary external bracing should then be added to each section before it is removed from the mock-up. Each section can then be removed when set, and further modified, as necessary, to provide flanges, etc., on the final moulding to provide rigidity at joint lines—e.g. see Fig. 22.9.

Final Mouldings

Making the final mouldings follows basic GRP lay-up technique. Generally two layers of $1\frac{1}{2}$ ($450g/m^3$) mat will provide adequate strength, but three layers may be preferred. Additional local reinforcement may be necessary in certain areas. Stiffeners may also be required, bonded to the underside of individual panels or sections. Attachment points for fitting to the chassis, local strengthening to take seats, etc., can also be bonded in while the moulding is still in the mould. A satisfactory ageing time must also be allowed in the mould so that there is no chance of the final mouldings distorting when removed from the mould.

CHAPTER TWENTY-THREE

Car body repairs

It is doubtful these days whether the home construction of GRP mouldings to replace damaged car bonnets or wings, etc., is a worthwhile proposition owing to the ready availability of commercially produced mouldings for most of the popular models. A damaged body unit, even if it can be removed intact, may need a considerable amount of work to re-build to a suitable shape to use as a pattern, from which a GRP female mould must then be taken before a final moulding can be produced. Ignoring the work involved, the cost alone may well approach that of a ready-made GRP moulding.

Relatively minor bodywork damage—and also deterioration through rusting—is a field where GRP products can prove particularly effective, and cost saving. In fact, patching with GRP, and filling in dents, has largely replaced the traditional repair methods of cutting and welding in new metal panels, and panel beating, even with professional repairs. The process is basically straightforward, but must be done with due attention to detail requirements if a 'clean' repair job is required, and the treatment is to be permanent.

Simple dents, scores and deep scratches are easily treated with resin/filler. The main requirement is to ensure that the area treated, and to which the resin/filler must adhere, is clean and durable. Ideally, the whole area should be wire brushed down to bare metal to ensure maximum ad-hesion. Resin/filler can be applied over paintwork (provided the surface has been degreased and de-waxed), but adhesion will then only be as good as that of the paint on the underlying body. Wax polishes are an obvious enemy of adhesion for they are release agents. Silicone waxes can also inhibit setting of the resin.

Resin Filler Mixes

A workable resin/filler mix can be produced from almost any laminating resin by mixing with talc to the consistency of a thick paste. However, such a mix will set very hard, making it difficult to trim off and finish flush with the surrounding surface. It may also tend to be quite brittle. This can result in cracking under vibrational or twisting loads on the repaired panel. Thus special filler pastes for car body repairs are normally based on flexible resins, which set 'softer' and are also much easier to flat down.

Resin/filler mix should be trowelled in place over a suitably prepared area, building up above the true body level. This is to allow for subsequent contraction on setting. If the dent is very deep it may be best to fill in two or three stages. Flatting down can be done towards the end of the hardening time, before the resin has reached its full hardness, using fine abrasive. Full details of how best to use a resin/body filler for car repair work are normally supplied with car repair kits and so do not need further description in detail here.

Repairs to Rust Damage

One of the most common repairs called for is to the bottom of doors or body sills where the metal has been eaten away with rust—and any remaining metal is frequently paper thin. The first step in the case of doors is to remove the interior lining panels (usually attached with screws and/or press-in fixes) so that the inside of the door panel itself is exposed. The whole area to be treated then needs brushing over thoroughly with a wire brush to remove all loose rust and loose corrosion products. It is not necessary to clean right down to a bright metal surface.

The outside of the door panel should now be treated in a similar way, and any unsupported metal edges remaining bent back to shape.

If the area to be repaired is relatively large it must be covered on the outside with a rigid backing, such as hardboard, sheet balsa or similar material cut to conform to the shape required and capable of being lashed or clamped in close contact with the outer surface of the door.

Before clamping up, a layer of thin acetate sheet should be placed between the door and the back-up material to act as a parting agent and give a nice smooth surface against which to lay the glass cloth or mat.

Small holes, etc., can be masked on the outside with Sellotape, simply using enough strips to cover all the holes completely to prevent the resin running through when applied from the inside— see Fig. 23.1.

Cloth or mat for the reinforcement is now cut to approximately the shape and size required, bearing in mind that this is to be laid in place on the inside surface of the door panel. Allow for two layers of cloth (or mat) as giving suitable thickness and rigidity.

Now apply resin generously to the inside of the door panel. Lay the first layer of glass cloth in place and brush resin well into it, jabbing with the brush to make sure that the cloth lies flat over the repair area and also that it is completely impregnated with resin—see Fig. 23.2. The latter is indicated by the fact that the glass will turn almost completely transparent when fully saturated. The second layer of glass cloth or mat can then be applied right over the first, again coating with resin. The whole job

FIG. 23.1

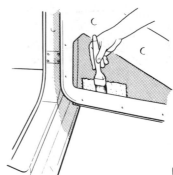

FIG. 23.2

can be left to set for at least 24 hours before attempting to peel off the Sellotape or remove the 'back-up' temporary structure.

The patch repair should now be quite hard and can be sanded down smooth prior to repainting to match the original colour of the door panel. If there is any roughness remaining, shallow spots can be filled with a resin/filler mix and sanded down. Small depressions are readily filled by 'knifing' in a resin/filler mix. Exactly the same treatment can, in fact, be used to fill in dents on bodywork, etc., instead of trying to knock them out. Simply level off with a resin/filler mix and sand down smooth when set.

Repairs to Cracked Wings (Fig. 23.3)

Repairs to cracked wings, etc., follow a similar technique in first brushing off rust, etc., from around the damaged area and then applying the resin/glass cloth 'patch' from the inside. In this case, however, there is usually no need to back up the front surface, as by closing up the crack there is little or no seepage of resin through. Instead, two pieces of board—each faced with a piece of acetate sheet or polythene sheet—should be clam-

ped up tight against the edge of the wing (on each side) to hold the two cracked portions together in their original position. This clamping up is done after the resin/cloth layers have been positioned. It will also be advisable to increase the number of laminations to three or four layers if the crack is at all extensive to get back to its original shape.

For applying the patches in really awkward places—e.g. right up inside a wing, or the top of a wheel arch where it may be difficult to get the layers to stay in place as you try to position them—the following technique is recommended. Lay a folded newspaper out over a flat surface and cover with a sheet of cellophane or polythene. Lay on a patch size of cloth and soak with resin. Add the second and further layers of glass cloth in the same way, impregnating each with resin in turn. The whole lot can now be picked up by putting one hand under the newspaper and simply placed in position over the patch area and smoothed and pressed into position. The whole patch area should, however, first be given a generous coat of resin which is allowed to gel off slightly to become tacky. Then the wet patch you picked up will have something to adhere to and will be easier to smooth out in

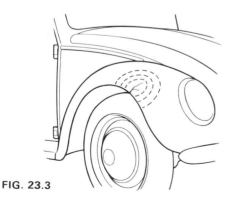

FIG. 23.3

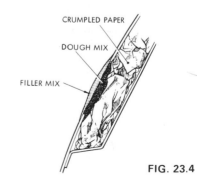

CRUMPLED PAPER

DOUGH MIX

FILLER MIX

FIG. 23.4

position. If necessary the whole patch can be held in position (e.g. if it shows any signs of falling away) with suitable props.

Other useful techniques include the use of fine-wire mesh to fill in large gaping holes before applying resin cloth layers, or simply resin/filler mix. Since the resin adheres strongly to metals (provided they are clean and grease-free) it can be used for sticking such metallic patches in place directly. A backing-up patch of cloth will be an advantage, if that side can be reached to apply it. Other areas requiring repair may be essentially 'hollow' and not accessible from the inside surface to apply the necessary patch—see Fig 23.4.

In this case a solution is to stuff the hollow interior out as far as possible with any suitable material—e.g. old newspapers crumpled up—and then apply a 'dough' mix through the hole to fill, as near as possible, to the original surface. Let the dough mix set and then make good and smooth up to surface level with resin/filler mix, finally sanding down smooth when hard.

In other cases it may be better practice to entirely re-make a panel or section, using the remains of the old part as a basic pattern or making a new pattern for the job. The replacement part in glass plastic can then be bonded in place with resin, or, if more suitable, bolted in position to the basic structure or attached with self-tapping screws, rivets, etc.

Once having acquired a certain basic knowledge in the application of glass plastics and resin/filler mixes, suitable methods of approach to almost any repair or replacement job will automatically suggest themselves. There is almost no limit to the extent to which glass fibre can be used for car bodywork repairs, although it cannot be recommended for repairs to stressed metal structural members which have fractured or broken, or for blanking off splits or holes in silencers.

CHAPTER TWENTY-FOUR

Repairs to GRP

Unless subject to bearing impact, damage to GRP mouldings is normally restricted to the gel coat. The bulk of the moulding itself is usually resilient enough to deform under excessive load but spring back in place unharmed when the load is removed. Only the gel coat is likely to suffer in such a case.

Gel Coat Repairs

Damage to the gel coat may appear in the form of a fine network of cracks, or from scratches or gouges, etc., produced by wear. In extreme cases where the moulding has been badly abraded whole areas of the gel coat may be worn away, exposing the ends of 'raw' glass fibres.

Gel coat crazing, or a network of cracks radiating from a single spot in the form of a 'sunburst' may be the result of faulty lay-up technique (Fig. 24.1). A more random distribution of cracks, forming a 'cobweb' pattern is usually the result of impact (Fig. 24.2). In this case tap the moulding in the damaged area to check the laminate for soundness. If it sounds dull, crack damage may have extended through the laminate instead of being confined to the gel coat. Repair in this case would call for backing up the moulding with another 'patch' layer or two of glass mat, as well as treating the cracks.

Fine cracks can be sealed by wiping over with activated resin. The crack pattern will still be visible, but the repair will effectively restore the seal originally provided by the undamaged gel coat.

Deeper cracks, or more pronounced cracks, can be opened slightly by scratching with the point of a knife, or a finely pointed tool, taking care not to dig too deep. They should then be filled in with resin/filler or resin putty, left slightly proud. When set, this should be levelled off flat and the whole area polished to restore the gloss. Again the repair will still be visible, for an exact match of colour is virtually impossible. However, the thin line of slightly different colour will usually be inconspicuous.

Deep scores and gouges are treated in a similar way, except that there is no need to scratch them out. A brushing with a wire brush is, however, advisable, to remove

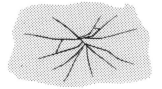 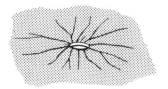

FIG. 24.1 GEL COAT CRAZING – Either from fault of technique or radiating from a stress point

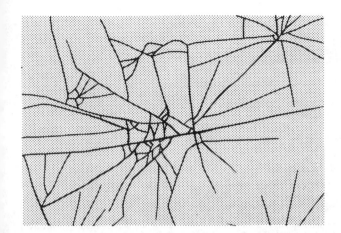

FIG. 24.2 'COBWEB' CRAZING—Normally resulting from impact

any surface dirt which may have accumulated in the score.

Small scratches, caused by rubbing, etc., may only be superficial, in which case they can often be polished right out, using an abrasive cleaner, metal polish or a burnishing paste. Try this first to see if it works. Very fine scratches which cannot be removed by polishing out may respond to painting with acetone, but do not let excess acetone spill on to the main surface as it is a solvent for polyester resin.

Chipped Edges

These are more difficult to repair neatly. The damaged edge surfaces should be roughened by wire brushing, when a new edge can be built up, slightly oversize, with pigmented resin/filler. Simple shuttering, bent from card and covered with cellophane, may be required to hold the filler in place until set. This can be secured in place with adhesive tape. If a stronger repair is needed, use a dough mix instead of resin/filler, polyester putty, or even epoxy resin.

Deeper Cavities

Provided the damage has not completely pierced the thickness of the moulding, these can be filled with resin/filler or dough mix, as appropriate. The mix used should be pigmented to match the gel coat colour as closely as possible.

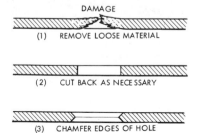

DAMAGE

(1)   REMOVE LOOSE MATERIAL

(2)   CUT BACK AS NECESSARY

(3)   CHAMFER EDGES OF HOLE

FIG. 24.3 PREPARATION OF HOLE DAMAGE FOR REPAIR

133

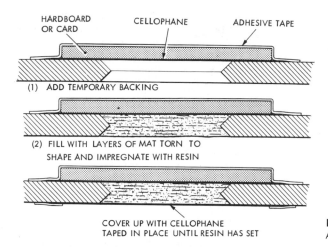

(1) ADD TEMPORARY BACKING

(2) FILL WITH LAYERS OF MAT TORN TO SHAPE AND IMPREGNATE WITH RESIN

COVER UP WITH CELLOPHANE TAPED IN PLACE UNTIL RESIN HAS SET

FIG. 24.4 STAGES IN FILLING A SMALL HOLE

Inspect the moulding on the other side. If this shows sign of damage, back up the repair with a patch layer of 1½ ounce (450g/m²) mat, applied with resin. The same back-up treatment may be needed in the case of deep scores and gouges.

Small Holes

When a moulding has been pierced right through the damage area will usually be further extended by cracks on the outer surface. The main job is to repair the principal damage first. Cracks can be filled in later, if necessary.

Cut the edges back in the form of a 'V', as shown (Fig. 24.3). Any completely loose material should be cut away, even if this means enlarging the hole. The damaged area should then be backed up on the outside with a piece of hardboard or stiff card, depending whether the surface is flat or curved, faced with acetate sheet. This can be held in place with adhesive tape (Fig. 24.4).

Working from the other side, brush on a gel coat first. Follow this by laying up small pieces of 1½ ounce (450g/m²) mat, torn to suitable size, and stippling in place until the required thickness has been built up. If more than four layers are needed, stop at the fourth layer and allow to gel and harden before proceeding with the next layers.

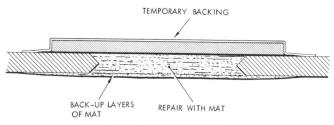

FIG. 24.5 LARGE HOLE REPAIR

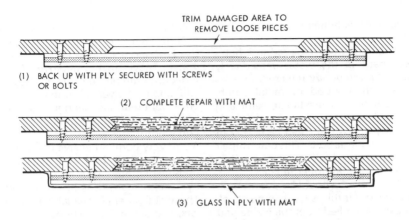

FIG. 24.6 TREATING MAJOR DAMAGE

Once completed properly a repair of this type should be as strong as the original material and will not need any back-up. The outer surface can be smoothed off and burnished, as necessary, to blend with the original surface, although colour matching will be virtually impossible. It may be necessary to paint over to tone in with the original colour.

Large Damaged Areas

Trim right back to undamaged material, regardless of the size of hole opened up. This should include cutting out any obviously deep cracks that run right through the thickness of the original moulding. Chamfer off the edges of the opening to a 'V' shape and fit shuttering on one side (preferably the outside). Repair then proceeds as above, using larger pieces of torn mat to build up to the required thickness. A back-up layer or two of mat, extending several inches either side of the original damage, should also be added in this case (Fig. 24.5).

An alternative method sometimes used on boat hulls, especially in regions where an interior patch will not show, is to back up the damaged area with a large piece of marine ply, glassed in (Fig. 24.6). This arrangement can also be used for a repair which does not conveniently lend itself to temporary shuttering, or where the shuttering cannot be placed on the outside. In this case a piece of marine ply is used for shuttering on the inside, and permanently fixed with bolts or screws. The hole damage is then made good from the outside, finishing smooth by filing and sanding down when set. The shuttering is then glassed over on the inside to hold it in place, the original fastenings for the ply usually being left in place.

Emergency Repairs to Boat Hulls

Emergency treatment may be necessary on a GRP boat hull to prevent water coming in through a damaged area. In this case the simplest, and obvious, treatment is to stuff rag, clothing, etc., into the hole to plug the leak, or if practical pull a sail or a polythene sheet against the hole from the outside. The latter treatment can be particularly

135

effective since polythene clings to a wet surface.

If the hull has to be repaired in a hurry and put back in the water immediately afterwards, a *temporary* repair can be attempted with a wood or metal patch, bedded down with mastic or paint and secured with through fasteners (i.e. bolts). Self tapping screws can also be used, but are not as reliable as bolts. This patch repair should be stripped off as soon as it is practical to make a proper repair.

Ideally the patch should be put on from the outside, but if this is quite impractical, then it can be applied from the inside and self tapping screws will have to be used.

Note some *epoxy resin* putties can be used under wet conditions, even under water. They can be employed for repair work on scratches, etc., on a boat which is still afloat. Polyester resins and normal GRP formulations cannot, however, be used in very damp conditions, and certainly not under water.

Note: Very comprehensive instructions on repairs to GRP hulls are available in a number of promotional booklets published by marine resin/paint manufacturers. These are generally available from chandlers, and some D.I.Y. shops.

The following photo-sequence shows typical treatment of repairs to damaged GRP boat hulls. (A similar method may be used for repairs to GRP car bodies, etc.)

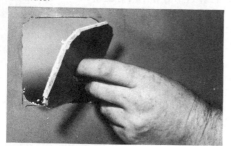

Mark out repair area clear of all damaged laminate.

Cut back to outline using a drill and padsaw.

Remove damaged laminate and check that surround is sound.

File from inside to form a wedge-shaped edge all round. Clean off dust.

Cut chopped strand mat to duplicate the original laminate, tailoring to area of hole.

Mat for backing laminate is cut increasing in size layer by layer.

Prepare flexible facia board larger than hole.

Drill matching bolt holes through hull.

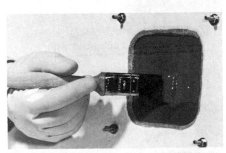

Coat inner surface of facia board with wax as release agent.

Bolt facia board to hull, pulling closely to contour.

Prepare and apply gel-coat to inner surface of board.

Allow gel-coat to cure then activate and mix lay-up resin.

Apply resin and position first layer of glass mat.

Stipple on more resin, then roll to consolidate and remove air.

Build up repair flush with inner surface and allow to cure.

Remove facia and fill bolt holes with resin putty.

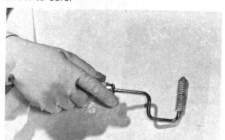

Apply backing laminate to interior of hull, covering repair.

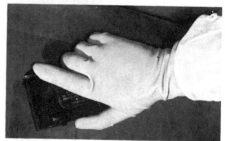

Blend in repair to outer contour of hull.

(Photo illustrations courtesy Fibreglass Ltd.)

CHAPTER TWENTY-FIVE

Faults—causes and remedies

A large proportion of the faults encountered in GRP mouldings are due to under-curing of the resin, often due to damp operating conditions, low ambient temperatures and/or the use of materials in the wrong proportions. The following covers possible faults, causes and remedies (or action to take next time if the fault is not curable!). Since faults can occur at various stages through production—and after —they are listed in separate categories.

1. GEL COAT STAGE

Fault		Cause	Remedy
Uneven coating with irregular bare patches	(i)	Mould surface contaminated	Wash mould surface with detergent and water—then polish
	(ii)	Wrong release agent	Avoid silicone polishes and/or release agents containing silicones
	(iii)	Contaminated gel coat resin	If sprayed, use an oil-free compressor
	(iv)	Wrong gel coat type	Change resin type
Sagging, uneven coat	(i)	Film too thick and heavy	Do not exceed film thickness of about 0.5 mm
	(ii)	Gel coat diluted	Do not dilute gel coat resin, unless recommended for the type used
Colour variation or mottled effect with coloured gel coat	(i)	Uneven brush application	Spraying is always better
	(ii)	Poor spray equipment and/or technique	Check—and practise technique
	(iii)	Poor atomisation	Reduce atomising air to a minimum
Colour streaking	(i)	Dirt in gel coat resin	Strain resin if suspect
	(ii)	Poor spraying technique	More practice!
	(iii)	Oil in compressed air supply	Use oil-free compressor
Gel coat remains tacky	(i)	Lack of catalyst or accelerator, or both	Check proportions, etc.
	(ii)	Wrong type of catalyst	
	(iii)	Unsuitable type of pigment	
	(iv)	Unsuitable type of filter	
	(v)	Damp mould	
	(vi)	Mould surface not sealed	
	(vi)	Wrong parting agent	

Gel coat only sets in patches

(i)   Damp mould

(ii) Catalyst not uniformly distributed — Stir well

(iii) Damp brush used to apply resin — Use only dry brush, but preferably spray

(iv) Presence of undried release agent on mould

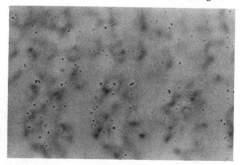

Pinholing

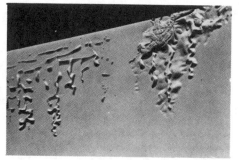

Wrinkling

2. FINISHED MOULDING WHEN REMOVED FROM MOULD

Fault	Cause	Remedy
Laminate remains sticky	(i) Lack of catalyst or accelerator or both	Use correct proportion
	(ii) Excessively low temperature	
	(iii) Damp atmosphere	
	(iv) Wrong type of filler (where used)	
	(v) Insufficient cure time in mould	
Pinholes in gel coat	(i) Air bubbles in gel coat film (brush application)	Too vigorous mixing of gel coat. Too vigorous brushing action
	(ii) Air bubbles in gel coat film (spray application)	Too much atomising air, resin over-thinned (avoid use of thinners even if this does make spraying easier)
	(iii) Gel coat not wetting on surface of release agent	Use PVA release agent in preference to wax types.
	(iv) Dirt on mould, or in gel coat resin	Keep dust off mould, open resin cans and release agent
	(v) Too much catalyst	Reduce proportion of catalyst
	(vi) Air entrained in filler or pigment	Use only fillers and pigments specified as suitable for the gel resin
	(vii) Forced cure	Always allow gel coat to cure at room temperature

Wrinkled (gel coat) surface	(i) Gel coat undercured	Check resin mix, operating conditions, etc.
	(ii) Gel coat too thin	Use thick coat—but not too thick
Fibre pattern shows through	(i) Gel coat too thin	Use thick coat—but not too thick
	(ii) Gel coat undercured	Allow more time for gel coat to cure before commencing lay-up
	(iii) Premature removal from mould	
Blistering	(i) Air pockets and air bubbles trapped in lay-up	Poor lay-up technique Resin proportion too low.
	(ii) Too much time between setting of gel coat and commencement of lay-up	
	(iii) Wrong type of gel coat resin	Make sure that lay-up resin is fully compatible with gel coat resin
Cratering	(i) As for blistering above	
	(ii) Soluble substances in release agent lifting gel coat from mould	Allow release agent to dry fully before applying gel coat

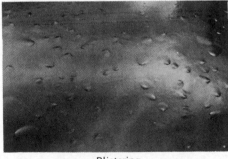

Blistering   Colour streaking

Tacky inside surface	(i) Final resin surface exposed to air has not cured	Improve operating conditions;
	(ii) Excessively damp atmosphere	check resins used Note: it may be possible to wash off this sticky resin with acetone, then apply a further coat of air-drying resin properly proportioned.
Moulding lacks hardness and rigidity	(i) Incomplete cure	Check resin mix (especially catalyst proportion) and working conditions

Poor opacity	(i)	Gel coat too thin— light shows through gel coat from laminate side	Use recommended maximum thickness of gel coat
	(ii)	Insufficient pigment in gel coat	Use higher proportion of pigment
Dry strands at top of moulding	(i)	Resin drainage	Use thixotropic resin on vertical surfaces
Moulding is distorted	(i)	Shrinkages (particularly likely on large flat areas)	Insufficient ribs or stiffeners incorporated. Moulding removed from mould before properly set
Moulding sticks in mould	(i)	Lack of parting agent	In some cases both PVA and wax may be necessary for suitable mould release
Sink marks	(i)	Shrinkage over a rib, former or insert	Allow laminate to cure partially before moulding in ribs or inserts
Hazing (foggy appearance of gel coat)	(i)	Incomplete cure of gel coat	Ensure gel coat is fully cured
	(ii)	Poor mould surface finish	Resurface mould
	(iii)	Poorly polished mould	Pay full attention to polishing

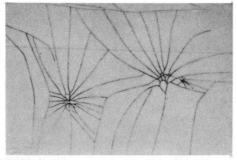

Cracked gel coat (star cracking)

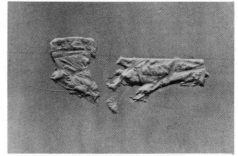

Flaking gel coat

3. FINISHED MOULDINGS AFTER AGEING

Fault		Cause	Remedy
Delamination	(i)	Insufficient resin and/or poor lay-up	Ensure adequate and even resin application
	(ii)	Poor wetting out	Make sure resin is suitable (e.g. could be of too high a viscosity)
	(iii)	Poor working conditions (e.g. dampness during lay-up)	
	(iv)	Use of damp materials	Glass mat, etc should always be stored in dry conditions

Flaking gel coat	(i)	Faulty adhesion between gel coat and lay-up	Avoid use of soft mould waxes which can penetrate the gel coat and affect adhesion
Star cracking of gel coat	(i)	Impact on reverse side of laminate	Use more flexible gel coat
Chalking	(i)	Incomplete cure (too much or too little catalyst)	No action possible at this stage
	(ii)	Degradation of pigment	Use colour-fast pigments
	(iii)	Surface breakdown due to exposure to atmosphere	Clean with detergent and water, then wax polish
Crazing (fine hairline cracks)	(i)	Gel coat too thin	Use most suitable type
	(ii)	Gel coat too brittle	of gel coat resin for service required, and at maximum recommended thickness
Fading and water-spotting	(i)	Incomplete cure of gel coat	No action possible at this stage
	(ii)	Unstable pigments	Surface colour can only restored by painting
Checking (crescent-shaped cracks appearing singly or in groups)	(i)	Trapped vapour blowing through gel coat on ageing	
Osmosis	(i)	Basically directly related to production conditions and technique	See Appendix 7

How thick?

Estimating Moulding Thickness

The thickness of a proposed GRP moulding using chopped strand mat can be predicted reasonably accurately knowing the total weight of mat and the resin to glass ratio. Total weight here refers to the actual weight of mat used multiplied by the numbers of layers. For any given *total* weight the final thickness should be the same, regardless of the actual combination weight–e.g. a *single* layer of 4 ounce mat (4oz/ft²) should give the same final thickness as *four* layers of 1 ounce mat (1oz/ft²), using the same proportion of resin in each case.

Reinforcement manufacturers now specify glass weights in grammes per square metre (g/m²) and thickness in millimetres (mm). In the U.K. both suppliers and users still normally prefer to work in English units. Simple conversions to remember are:–

glass weight in g/m² × .0033 = oz/ft²
glass weight in oz/ft² × 300 = g/m²

Normal thickness equivalents are:–

in	$\frac{1}{64}$	$\frac{1}{32}$	$\frac{3}{64}$	$\frac{1}{16}$	$\frac{3}{32}$
mm	0.4	0.8	1.2	1.5	2.5

in	$\frac{1}{8}$	$\frac{5}{32}$	$\frac{3}{16}$	$\frac{1}{4}$	$\frac{3}{8}$
mm	3	4	5	6	10

The following table gives laminate thickness for different resin to glass ratios in both English and metric units.

TABLE A1   THICKNESS OF CSM LAMINATES

Resin to glass by weight		3:1	2½:1	2¼:1	2:1	1½:1	1:1
Resin content % by weight		75	72	70	$66\frac{2}{3}$	60	50
glass weight oz/ft²	g/m²	thickness mm and nominal inch fraction equivalent					
1	300	0.87 ($\frac{1}{32}$)	0.75 ($\frac{1}{32}$)	0.69	0.62	0.50	0.37 ($\frac{1}{64}$)
1½	450	1.13 ($\frac{3}{64}$)	1.13 ($\frac{3}{64}$)	1.03	0.94	0.74 ($\frac{1}{32}$)	0.56
2	600	1.75	1.50 ($\frac{1}{16}$)	1.37	1.25	0.99	0.74 ($\frac{1}{32}$)
2½	750	2.18	1.57 ($\frac{5}{14}$)	1.72	1.56 ($\frac{1}{16}$)	1.24 ($\frac{3}{64}$)	0.93
3	900	2.63 ($\frac{3}{32}$)	2.25 ($\frac{3}{32}$)	2.06	1.87	1.49 ($\frac{1}{16}$)	1.11 ($\frac{3}{64}$)
4	1200	3.50 ($\frac{9}{64}$)	3.0 ($\frac{1}{8}$)	2.75 ($\frac{7}{64}$)	2.50 ($\frac{3}{32}$)	2.0	1.48 ($\frac{1}{16}$)
5	1500	4.36 ($\frac{11}{64}$)	3.75 ($\frac{9}{64}$)	3.45 ($\frac{9}{64}$)	3.12 ($\frac{1}{8}$)	2.5 ($\frac{3}{32}$)	1.86
6	1800	5.26 ($\frac{13}{64}$)	4.50 ($\frac{11}{64}$)	4.12	3.75	3.0	2.22 ($\frac{3}{32}$)
8	2400	7.00	6.0 ($\frac{1}{4}$)	5.50 ($\frac{7}{32}$)	5.00	4.0 ($\frac{5}{32}$)	3.00 ($\frac{1}{8}$)
10	3000	8.72 ($\frac{11}{32}$)	7.5 ($\frac{5}{16}$)	6.90	6.25 ($\frac{1}{4}$)	5.0	3.75 ($\frac{5}{32}$)

Simple Calculation

A quick and easy method of estimating laminate thickness using the normal resin to glass ratio of around $2\frac{1}{2}$ to 1 for hand lay-up is to use a figure of $\frac{1}{32}$ in for each ounce/ft² of matt. For example, if the final laminate uses four layers of $1\frac{1}{2}$ ounce mat $= 4 \times 1\frac{1}{2}$ or 6 oz/ft² of glass, the thickness will be $6 \times \frac{1}{32}$ or $\frac{3}{16}$ in.

A more accurate estimation of laminate thickness can be based on the following figures for a 2:1 resin glass ratio:–
(i)   Thickness $= 0.024$ in per oz/ft² glass.
(ii) Thickness $= 0.20$ mm per 100g/m² glass.

Thus for four layers of $1\frac{1}{2}$ ounce mat (6 oz/ft² of glass), estimated thickness is $6 \times .024 = 0.144$ in.

This will be the thickness for a 2:1 resin glass ratio. For any other resin:glass ratio, factor this formula thickness by the actual resin:glass ratio/2. Thus if the resin:glass

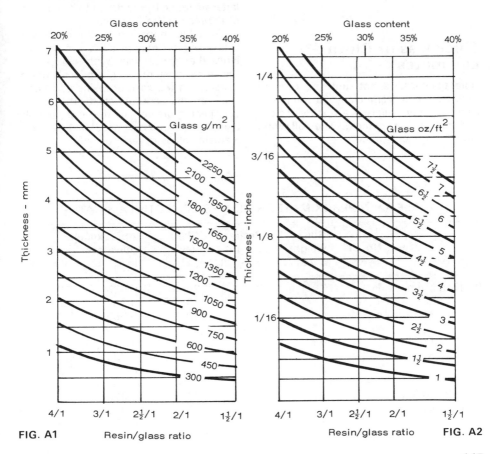

FIG. A1   Resin/glass ratio

Resin/glass ratio   FIG. A2

ratio is 2.5, the thickness in this case becomes:—

2.5/2×0.144=0.18 in.

For working in metric units, use the second formula in the same way.

An even simpler method is to read laminate thickness from graphs—see Figs. A1 and A2.

Thickness of Cloth Laminates

Here thickness is not quite so easy to estimate simply, particularly if a composite laminate is involved (e.g. a mixture of cloth and mat and/or rovings). The following table is a general guide.

Thickness of any Laminate

If you do not mind a little calculation the thickness of *any* laminate can be estimated quite accurately, based on using the *thickness constant* for the various materials involved together with their respective proportions. Since all the materials contribute bulk to the final laminate, the thickness of the laminate is then the sum of the individual material weights multiplied by their thickness constant. Values of the latter are found by dividing 1 by the density of the material(s) involved.

The table opposite gives thickness constants for most materials likely to be used. Note that these vary with density, so thickness constants are given for a range of densities in the case of resins and fillers. Use the value appropriate to the density (or specific gravity) of the resin actually being used. Adjust as necessary for intermediate values of resin density.

TABLE A2   APPROXIMATE THICKNESS OF CLOTH LAMINATES

Material	No. of layers	Glass weight oz/sq. ft	Resin weight oz/sq. ft	Glass: Resin (%)	Approximate thickness in	mm
0.015 in scrim	1	1	2	30	0.035	0.9
	2	2	3	30	0.050	1.25
	4	4	5.5	40	0.085	2.2
Cloth (0.009 in close weave)	1	0.8	0.6	60	0.015	0.4
	2	1.6	1.2	60	0.030	0.8
	4	3.2	2.4	60	0.060	1.5
Cloth (0.010 in open weave)	1	0.8	1.2	40	0.020	0.5
	2	1.6	2.4	40	0.035	1.0
	4	3.2	3.6	45	0.055	1.5

TABLE A3   THICKNESS FOR LAMINATE MATERIALS

Material	Specific Gravity	Density ounces/ft *or* kg/m²	Thickness constant English units	metric units
Glass fibre 'E' glass	2.55	2.56	.00461	.391
'S' glass	2.50	2.50	.00473	.400
'C' glass	2.45	2.45	.00482	.408
Kevlar 49	1.45	1.45	.00816	.690
Carbon fibre HS	1.74	1.74	.00680	.575
Carbon fibre HM	1.81	1.81	.00617	.552
Polyester fabric	1.38	1.38	.00858	.725
Polyester resin	1.1	1.1	.01075	.909
	1.2	1.2	.00985	.833
	1.3	1.3	.00860	.769
	1.4	1.4	.00845	.714
Epoxy resin	1.1	1.1	.01075	.909
	1.3	1.3	.00860	.769
Fillers	2.3	2.3	.00515	.435
	2.5	2.5	.00473	.400
	2.9	2.9	.00410	.345

Notes:

(i)   Using *English* units, the thickness constant multiplied by the material weight in oz/ft² gives thickness in *inches per 1 oz/ft² of the material.*

Using *metric* units the thickness constant multiplied by the material weight in kg/m² gives thickness in *millimetres* per 1 kg/m² of the material.

(ii)   To calculate the thickness constant for any other material:—
In English units: thickness constant = .0018 × material weight (oz/ft²)
In metric units: thickness constant
$$= \frac{1}{\text{material weight (kg/m}^3)}$$
The following examples should make the method of calculation clear.

Example 1A: A laminate consists of 4 oz/ft² chopped strand mat in 'E' glass and polyester resin (specific gravity 1.2) with a resin:glass ratio of $2\frac{1}{4}$:1.
Thickness of glass = glass weight ×
(English) thickness factor for glass
= 4 × .004610 = .0184 in
Weight of resin = $2\frac{1}{4}$ × glass weight
= $2\frac{1}{4}$ × 4 = 9 oz/ft²
∴ Thickness of resin = glass weight ×
(English) thickness factor for resin
= 9 × .00985 = .08865 in
Total thickness = glass thickness + resin thickness
= .0184 + .08865 = *.10705 in*

Example 1B: A laminate consists of 1200 g/m² chopped strand mat in 'E' glass and polyester resin (specific gravity 1.2) with a resin:glass ratio of $2\frac{1}{4}$:1.
Note: This is the same as example 1A,

but expressed in metric units.

Thickness of glass=glass weight×
    (metric) thickness factor for glass
    $=1.2 \times .391 = .470$ mm

Thickness of resin=resin weight×
(metric) thickness factor for resin
    $=2\frac{1}{4} \times 1.2 \times .833 = 2.250$ mm

Total thickness=glass thickness+resin
    thickness
    $=.470+2.250 = 2.720$ mm

Note that when working in *metric* units the glass weight, normally expressed in *grammes* per square metre (g/m²), must be rendered as *kilogrammes* per sq. metre (kg/m²).

Example II. A laminate consists of 1 layer of 'E' glass 1 oz/ft² mat and 4 layers of 2 oz/ft² 'E' glass mat. The resin mix con-sists of 60 parts by weight polyester resin (specific gravity 1.2) and 40 parts by weight filler (specific gravity 2.5). Resin: glass ratio is $2\frac{1}{2}$:1.

Weight of glass$=1+4 \times 2 = 9$ oz/ft²
. ˙. Thickness of glass$=9 \times .00461 =$
    .0415 in

Weight of resin$=2\frac{1}{2} \times$ weight of glass
    $=2\frac{1}{2} \times 9 = 22.5$ oz/ft²
. ˙. Thickness of resin$=22.5 \times .00985$
    $=.2216$ in

Weight of filler$=40/60 \times$ weight of
    resin
    $=40/60 \times 22.5 = 15$ oz/ft²
. ˙. Thickness of filler$=15 \times .00473$
    $=.710$ in

Total thickness$=.0415+.2216+.0710$
    $=.334$ in

APPENDIX TWO

How strong?

The strength of a GRP laminate (or an RP laminate) is difficult to specify exactly since it will vary with the type of reinforcement, its directional properties and the resin-to-glass ratio, further modified by the actual method of producing the laminate. Thus in hand lay-up mouldings the final strength can vary with different people doing this work.

Reinforcement materials can be divided into three groups–undirectional, bidirectional and random. Rovings, for example, are unidirectional; the fibres are orientated to give maximum strength in one direction. Woven fabrics are bidirectional; weaving lays strands in two different directions, but may have greater strength in one direction than another. Chopped strand mat is random; its fibres are orientated at random producing roughly uniform strength in all directions. However, its actual strength is much lower than that of rovings or woven fabrics because the fibres are short and more easily torn apart.

As regards the resin-to-glass ratio, glass fibre is much stronger than resin so, logically, the greater the proportion of glass in the laminate the greater the strength. However, there are practical limits to the *amount* of resin which can be used with different laminates–typically 20-40% with uni-directional reinforcement (rovings), 40-60% with bidirectional reinforcement (woven fabrics) and 60-75% with chopped strand mat. Any lower resin content would not wet out the glass properly and higher resin content would merely represent excess resin and further loss of

TABLE A4   MECHANICAL PROPERTIES*

Material	Glass content by weight %	Specific Gravity	Tensile strength MN/m²	Tensile modulus GN/m²	Compressive strength MN/m²	Compressive modulus GN/m²	Flexural strength MN/m²	Flexural modulus GN/m²	In-plane shear strength MN/m²	In-plane shear modulus GN/m²
Uni directional										
Wound epoxide	60–90	1.7–2.2	530–1730	28–62	310–480		690–1860	34–48		
Uni-directional polyester	50–75	1.6–2.0	410–1180	21–41	210–480		690–1240	27–41		
Bi-directional										
Satin weave polyester	50–70	1.6–1.9	250–400	14–25	210–280	9–17	207–450	17–23	62–83	3.5–4.0
Woven roving polyester	45–60	1.5–1.8	230–340	13–17	98–140	8–17	200–270	10–17	55–76	3.0–3.5
Random										
Preform polyester	25–50	1.4–1.6	70–170	6–12	130–160		70–240			
Hand and spray up polyester	25–40	1.4–1.5	63–140	6–12	130–170	6–9	140–250	5–8	69–83	2.8–3.0
Moulding Compounds										
DMC polyester	10–40	1.8–2.0	34–70	12–14	140–180		40–140		41–69	
SMC polyester	20–35	1.8–1.85	50–90	9	240–310		140–210	9–14	65–83	
Glass filled nylon	20–40	1.3–1.5	120–200	6–14	110–170					
Thermoplastics										
High density polyethylene	0	0.95	31	0.6–1	17		7	0.7		
High impact polystyrene	0	1.08	45	3.5	112		90	2.7–3.4		
Polypropylene	0	0.9	40	1.1–1.8	60–70		34–55	0.8–1.8		
Nylon	0	1.08	80	1.4–1.8	35–91		55–97	1.4–2.8		
Foam										
Polyurethane	0	0.035	0.3	0.0041	0.15–0.2	.0014–.003			0.172	0.0015
Metals										
Mild steel		7.8	410–480	210	410–480					
Aluminium		2.7	80–430	70	84					
Stainless steel		7.92	480–1580	200						

*Fibreglass Limited

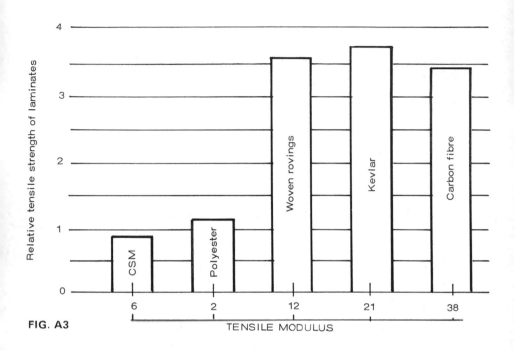

FIG. A3   TENSILE MODULUS

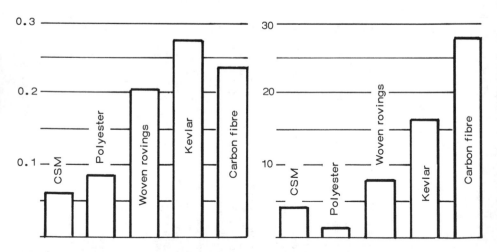

FIG. A4   SPECIFIC STRENGTH

strength. It follows, therefore, that uni-directional reinforcement is not only stronger to start with, but gives laminates which have further improved strength as a result of their lower resin content.

Table A4 presents a summary of typical sectional properties of different types of GRP laminates, together with that of some other materials for comparison. Values are given in metric units. For conversion into English units use the following:

MN/m² multiplied by 0.15 = lb/m²
GN/m² multiplied by 150 = lb/m²

Comparing Glass Fibre with other Fabrics

Fig. A.3 compares, diagrammatically, the comparative tensile strength of GRP laminates with similar hand lay-up laminates produced using the same (polyester) resin with polyester, Kevlar and carbon fibre. Of these only Kevlar shows up as slightly superior to glass fibre in actual (laminate) tensile strength, but on a *modulus* basis both are markedly superior with carbon fibre coming out well on top. Fig. A.4

shows the performance of these different types of reinforcements on a specific strength and specific modulus basis—i.e. comparing performance on a weight-for-weight basis.

Basically these diagrams show that where maximum strength of laminate is the main concern, both Kevlar and carbon fibre can offer a superior performance over glass rovings. Normally, however, the much higher price of these reinforcement materials excludes them from normal applications, i.e. where cost is more important than absolute performance.

How GRP behaves under Stress

It is interesting to compare the behaviour of GRP laminates under stress. As Fig. A.5 shows, a stress/strain curve for GRP is linear, up to the point of ultimate failure. This is quite different from the behaviour of common metals which, although having a steeper curve, show a yield point at which the metal becomes 'elastic' and stretches rapidly with little further increase in stress.

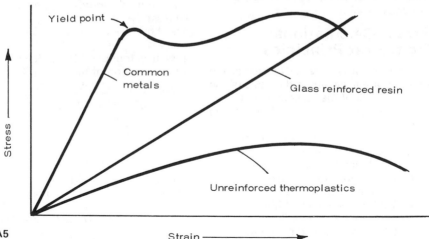

FIG. A5

This yield point designates the effective failure point of the metal. This explains why a GRP moulding will not be dented under impact (like a metal panel). It will either spring back to its original shape, or fail by cracking if the localised impact load is greater than the strength of the GRP.

The behaviour of unreinforced thermoplastic materials, also shown in the table, is quite different again. They are 'elastic' materials which elongate readily under increasing tensile stress. Also their strength is temperature dependent, decreasing markedly with increasing temperature.

'Balancing' a Laminate

Theoretically, at least, a 'balanced' laminate would be one where both the fibres and the resin are strained to the same extent. In other words the ratio of stress at failure to elastic modulus of both the fibres and the resin should be balanced. This question is largely academic however, for glass fibres have an elastic modulus 20 times greater than polyester resin, and in a laminate can thus carry 20 times the stress. For most practical purposes, therefore, the contribution of the resin stress is negligible by comparison.

Stress Calculations from First Principles

Nevertheless it is possible to predict the strength of a laminate on the basis of the tensile moduli of the components, viz.

$$E_L = E_f.V_f.ß + E_r.V_r \qquad \text{formula (1)}$$

when

E_L = tensile modulus of the laminate
E_f = tensile modulus of the fibres
E_r = tensile modulus of the resin
V_f = volume fraction of fibres
V_r = volume fraction of resin
ß = 1.0 for unidirectional fibres
= 0.5 for bidirectional fibres
= 0.375 for chopped strand mat

To use this formula it is first necessary to express resin-to-glass ratio in terms of *volume fraction* rather than percentage weight, as normally quoted in GRP work. To do this another formula is used:—

$$V_f = \frac{W_f/\triangle f}{W_f/\triangle f + W_r/\triangle r} \qquad \text{formula (2)}$$

where W_f is the weight fraction of the fibre
$\triangle f$ is the density of the fibre
W_r is the *weight fraction* of the resin
$\triangle r$ is the density of the resin

Having found the volume fraction of the fibre (V_f) content in this way, the volume fraction of the resin (V_r) follows as $1-V_f$.

A worked out example should make it clear how to use these formulas, considering a chopped strand mat laminate with a 3:1 resin to glass ratio in polyester resin. Fibre density is given as $2.6\,kg/m^3$, and resin density $1.2\,kg/m^3$. Elastic modulus of the fibre (E_f) is $68950\ MN/m^2$. Elastic modulus of polyester resin (Ev) is $3447\ MN/m^2$. (Note: manufacturers now quote material property, etc., entirely in metric units and so these will be used here).

Set out the figures in terms of weight expressed as a fraction:—

glass fibre $= \frac{1}{3}$ $= .33$
resin $= \frac{2}{3}$ $= .67$

Now use formula (2) to determine the volume fraction of the fibre:—

$$V_f = \frac{.33/2.56}{.33/2.56 + .67/1.2}$$

$$= \frac{.129}{.129 + .56}$$

$$= .187$$

V_r then follows as $1 - .187 = .813$

Now use formula (1) to determine the tensile modulus of the complete laminate:—

$$E_L = 68950 \times .187 \times .375 + 3447 \times .813$$

$$=4835+2802$$
$$=7637 \text{ MN/m}^2$$

These formulas can be used to estimate the performance of virtually any laminate, even those including fillers. In that case formula (1) remains the same (the fillers do not add any strength). Formula (2) must be extended to take into account the effect of filler proportion on the respective volume fractions of fibre and resin, i.e.

$$V_f = \frac{W_f/\triangle_f}{W_f/\triangle_f + W_r/\triangle_r + W_x/\triangle_x}$$

$$\text{and } V_r = \frac{W_r/\triangle_r}{W_f/\triangle_f + W_r/\triangle_r + W_x/\triangle_x}$$

where W_x = weight of filler
$\triangle_x$ = density of filler

Useful property values to use in calculations are given in Table A4A.

TABLE A4A TYPICAL PROPERTY VALUES (See also Table A4)

Type of laminate	Density of fibres	Density of resin	Elastic modulus E_f	E_r
Unidirectional	2.56	1.2	68900	3445
Chopped strand mat	2.56	1.2	68900	3445
Woven rovings	2.56	1.2	68900	3445

APPENDIX THREE

How heavy?

TABLE A5   WEIGHT OF LAMINATES

	Resin-to-glass ratio					
	3:1	$2\frac{1}{2}$:1	$2\frac{1}{4}$:1	2:1	$1\frac{1}{2}$:1	1:1
By weight %	75	72	70	$66\frac{2}{3}$	60	50

glass weight		moulding weight oz/ft (kg/m²)					
oz/ft²	g/m²						
1	300	4 (1.2)	$3\frac{1}{2}$ (1.5)	$3\frac{1}{4}$(0.975)	3 (0.9)	$2\frac{1}{2}$ (0.83)	2 (0.6)
$1\frac{1}{2}$	450	6 (1.8)	$5\frac{1}{4}$ (1.6)	$4\frac{7}{8}$ (1.9)	$4\frac{1}{2}$ (1.39)	$3\frac{3}{4}$ (1.1)	3 (0.9)
2	600	8 (2.4)	7 (2.1)	$6\frac{1}{2}$ (1.99)	6 (1.8)	5 (1.9)	4 (1.2)
$\frac{1}{2}$	750	10 (3.0)	$8\frac{3}{4}$ (2.6)	$8\frac{1}{8}$ (2.45)	$7\frac{1}{2}$ (2.25)	$6\frac{1}{4}$(1.879)	5 (1.5)
3	900	$10\frac{1}{2}$ (3.19)	$9\frac{3}{4}$ (3.0)	9 (2.7)	9 (2.7)	$7\frac{1}{2}$ (2.25)	6 (1.8)
4	1200	16 (4.8)	14 (4.2)	13 (3.9)	12 (3.6)	10 (3.0)	8 (2.4)
5	1500	20 (6.0)	$17\frac{1}{2}$ (9.25)	$16\frac{1}{4}$ (4.9)	15 (4.5)	$12\frac{1}{2}$ (3.79)	10 (3.0)
6	1800	24 (7.2)	21 (6.3)	$19\frac{1}{2}$ (9.85)	18 (5.4)	15 (4.5)	12 (3.6)
8	2400	32 (9.6)	28 (8.9)	26 (7.8)	24 (7.2)	20 (6.0)	16 (4.8)
10	3000	40 (24.0)	35 (10.9)	$32\frac{1}{2}$ (9.79)	30 (9.0)	25 (7.5)	20 (6.0)

The basic rule in estimating the weight of a GRP moulding is that nothing is 'lost' by the glass and resin, and nothing is 'added' by the setting process—so the finished weight of the moulding is the sum of the glass and resin weights actually used. In a practical moulding there is, of course, also the weight of the gel coat although the actual proportion contributed to total weight is small enough to be ignored. Where fillers are used, however, these can add appreciable extra weight, computed simply as weight of filler.

In the case of chopped strand mat mouldings, the foregoing table gives laminate weights for different resin to glass ratios.

APPENDIX FOUR

GRP resistance to chemicals etc.

Basically the resistance of GRP to attack by chemicals, etc. is the same as that of the resin used. Polyester resin is by far the most used resin and has generally excellent resistance to most substances which would attack metals, including acids, and is fully resistant to oils and hydrocarbon fuels, etc. In other words, with polyester GRP mouldings one would not normally expect any 'corrosion' or degradation problems.

There are, however, certain substances against which polyester resins offer only poor resistance and others for which they are not recommended. In such cases use of a different resin (epoxy or furane) can provide a better or fully suitable answer. Here is a 'danger list' for polyester resins, with alternatives which can be used in each case. The resistance of the alternative resin(s) is designated G for good or E for excellent.

Polyester resins are POOR with:
acetic acid—use furane (G).
benzene—use epoxy (E) or furane (E).

Polyester resins are NOT recommended with:
acetone—use furane (G); epoxy is also *not* recommended.
ammonium hydroxide—use epoxy (E) or furane (E).
aniline—use furane (G); epoxy is also *not* recommended.
carbon bisulphide—use furane (E).
chloroform—use epoxy (E) or furane (E).
ether—use furane (E).
ethyl acetate—use furane (E); epoxy is also *not* recommended.
formic acid—use furane (G).
lime—use epoxy (E) or furane (E).
methyl acetate—use furane (E); epoxy is also *not* recommended.
methyl ethyl ketone—use furane (E); epoxy is also *not* recommended.
nitrobenzene—use furane (E).
nitromethane—use furane (E).
phenol—use furane (E); epoxy is also *not* recommended.
potassium hydroxide—use epoxy (E) or furane (E).
sodium hydroxide—use epoxy (E) or furane (E).
trichloroethylene—use furane (E).

Ageing effects

Is GRP a completely durable material free from degradation with age and loss of strength from fatigue (like most metals)? Experience has shown that for most practical purposes it is. Boat hulls moulded in GRP nearly twenty five years ago are still sound, though gel coats may have discoloured or crazed in places. Ignoring actual mechanical damage, GRP can be regarded as a fully durable material. Any failure through delamination, or loss of properties through osmosis, is traceable to *production* faults and not GRP itself, provided the design was right in the first place.

Having said that, some qualification is needed. GRP *does* suffer a loss of properties with age although as regards mechanical strength this is more than accommodated by the safety factor adopted in the original design. Specifically, being a visco-elastic material it is subject to *creep* and *fatigue* which can result in progressive loss of flexural strength and ultimate strength, respectively.

The effect of *creep* is shown diagrammatically in Fig. A6 for a typical CSM laminate. Two main factors affect the loss of flexural strength – temperature and im-

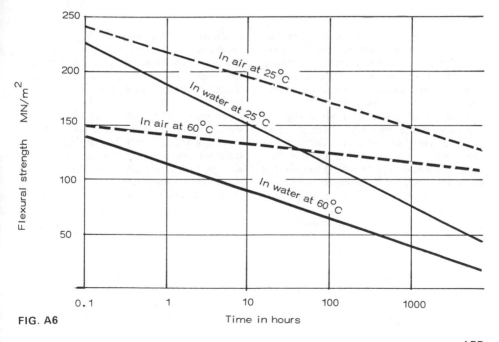

FIG. A6

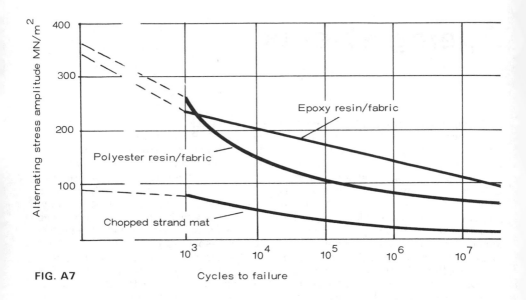

FIG. A7   Cycles to failure

mersion in water. In the short term, an increase in temperature can markedly reduce the flexural strength, but in the long term the effect is reversed in air. Immersed in water there is a continual loss of flexural strength at any temperature.

The effect of *fatigue* is shown in Fig. A7. Here curves are drawn for three different kinds of laminate—polyester/CSM, polyester/fabric and epoxy/fabric. The two fabric laminates have about the same initial strength, but polyester/fabric suffers a more gradual loss of ultimate strength due to fatigue. The fatigue performance of all three, however, compares favourably with most metals.

Finally, the ageing effect which is most likely to be noticed—the effect of weathering. This is degradation of the surface on the side exposed to weathering action, i.e. normally the gel coat. In outdoor atmospheres the gel coat can be expected to lose

its gloss over the years, although this can be recovered by *very* lightly abrading off and wax polishing as long as the gel coat is not eventually worn through. The best durability will be found in gel coats chosen to provide adequate resistance to water absorption and erosion (and a backing of surfacing tissue also helps prolong the 'new' life of a gel coat). The laminates most resistant to weathering, too, are those with a high proportion of resin on the side exposed to weathering.

Fading, chalking or loss of colour is another characteristic of weathering, but this is due to inadequate pigment properties (also some colours—particularly reds—are more prone to 'chalk' or fade on exposure to light). On an impigmented translucent laminate, normal ageing will tend to darken appearance (i.e. produce loss of translucency). If this is to be minimised, UV stabilised resins must be used.

Thermal properties of GRP laminates

GRP laminates expand and contract more than metals under changes in temperature, but this normally presents no problems. Metals, on the other hand, conduct heat better than GRP, so in this respect GRP mouldings are better heat insulators.

The mechanical properties of GRP laminates are not appreciably affected by changes in temperature, although there is a recommended maximum service temperature above which properties are degraded. GRP laminates can readily withstand very low temperatures and, in fact, may actually show an increase in strength at low temperatures.

TABLE A6   THERMAL PROPERTIES OF GRP LAMINATES

Laminate	Coefficients of		Maximum Service Temperature
	Thermal Expansion deg. $C \times 10^{-6}$	Thermal Conductance W/m deg. C	
UNI DIRECTIONAL			
wound−epoxy	4−11	0.31−0.59	260°C
wound−polyester	5−11	0.31−0.56	260°C
BI DIRECTIONAL			
satin weave fabric−polyester	7−12	0.26−0.36	180°C
woven roving−polyester	11−16	0.27−0.31	180°C
RANDOM			
CSM−polyester hand lay-up	22−36	6.24−0.28	180°C
CSM−polyester spray-up	24−40	6.23−0.25	170°C
MOULDING COMPOUND			
DMC−polyester	14−22	0.31−0.36	230°C
SMC−polyester	14−22	0.28−0.34	230°C

Osmosis

Osmosis is a form of blistering normally only found on the underwater parts of GRP boat hulls. Its appearance is random and it affects only a proportion of GRP boats, but sufficient in numbers to have caused considerable concern and precipitated (often unnecessary) very expensive treatment to remedy. The *cause* is invariably some deficiency in the production of the original laminate (e.g. using unsuitable resins, working in poor conditions, or faulty lay-up work, etc.), generating voids which are filled by free styrene. No resins are completely waterproof, they all absorb a certain amount of moisture in time. Subsequent penetration of moisture into these void areas can then build up considerable pressure, lifting the gel coat in the immediate vicinity into a blister.

Whole areas of blistering may occur, but not because the 'disease' is spreading like measles. It will only occur on areas where the cause is already there, and develop into blistering over a period of time. The *effect*, however, is often exaggerated. Small blisters which appear and then do not grow any more are only a cosmetic defect. They will not have any effect on the strength of the laminate or on the protection provided by the gel coat, unless very widespread and densely located. In fact blisters less than about $\frac{1}{5}$in (5mm) diameter are best left alone. No remedial treatment is necessary unless there are cosmetic reasons (which are largely unlikely on a part of a hull normally not seen).

Some osmotic blisters, on the other hand, may continue to grow in size. The blister skin of gel coat is then very prone to be broken, exposing the laminate below to water penetration. Thus blisters which are broken, or large blisters which can easily be broken (e.g. with fingernail pressure) need remedial treatment. If there is an obvious cavity, treatment is certainly necessary, as this will probably show as an area of 'dry' glass which will readily absorb water and draw it into the laminate. Treatment involves removing the unsupported area of gel coat (the actual blister), thoroughly washing out and drying the cavity. The whole cavity can then be refilled with epoxy resin stopping compound. (Polyester stopping compound can be used but is not as good). After hardening this is flattened down and a final coat of epoxy paint applied over the area.

There is another type of blister which can develop. It is broad and flat and not always spotted unless viewed from along the surface of the laminate, or detected as a raised area when a finger is rubbed over it. Actual size of the affected area may range up to 2in (50mm) diameter. In this case the void causing the trouble is located in the laminate itself, not just under the gel coat, and there is no thin blister surface which can easily be removed. The whole area needs to be dug out to expose the extent of the void which, after cleaning and drying, needs to be filled first with CSM and resin to rebuild to the full thickness of the laminate, followed by epoxy stopping compound for the final surfacing.

Large blisters of this type most certainly need remedial treatment when detected for they can continue to grow under osmotic pressure and weaken the laminate itself.

Resin technology

Polyesters are formed by reacting an organic debasic (carboxylic) acid with a glycol. The resulting product is a *thermoplastic* resin which is solid at room temperatures and is used in this form to make textile fibres (e.g. Terylene in Britain and Dacron in the U.S.A.).

If the debasic acid is *unsaturated,* addition of a suitable catalyst to this form of polyester in a molten state will set it as a hard, unfusible solid. In other words, the catalyst has turned the original polyester resin into a *thermoset* material. However, whilst hard, it is far too brittle for commercial use. Thus most *thermosetting* polyester resins are based on a mixture of saturated and unsaturated debasic acids, the mixture being adjusted as required to produce the required properties. In addition a third component—usually styrene—is used to render the resin in liquid form and further control the final structure of the cured resin. The majority of commercial polyester resins are produced as solutions of reactive polyester in styrene.

It is the unsaturated polyester part of the composition which contains the reactive groups and the final properties of the resin can be varied by changing its composition. A decrease in the proportion of unsaturated acid reduces the reactivity of the polyester and makes it more flexible and more water resistant. At the same time it reduces chemical resistance and lowers the heat diabatic temperature.

The *reactive* acid component is almost invariably maleic. Various different *non-reactive* acids may be used and these have a further modifying effect on the properties. The usual choice is phthalic anhydride. If this is replaced with iso-phthalic acid, the cured resin has an improved flexural modulus, better resistance to crazing, better resistance to water and a higher heat diabatic temperature. Isophthalic type resin, therefore, would be a logical choice for a gel coat. It is, however, more expensive to produce.

Different glycols can also be used, further modifying the final properties of the resin when cured. Complex glycols are commonly used to improve chemical resistance and/or heat resistance. Resins formulated on this basis are known as *bispherol polyesters*. Where optimum resistance to hot water and detergent solutions is required, standard resins with a high *maleic* content are used.

In the case of fire-resistant polyester resins, flammability is commonly reduced by the use of resin components containing high proportions of chlorine or bromine; also by incorporating chlorowaxes as additives.

Styrene, basically, is the solvent for polyester (as well as being a cross linking monomer in the actual resin structure), rendering the resin in solutions of handleable viscosity.

Deflections and stresses in sandwich laminates

The formula giving the flexural rigidity (R) of a sandwich beam simply supported at the ends and bonded at the centre (Fig. A8) is:–

$$R = \frac{E.b.(T^3 - c^3)}{12}$$

where
  E is the elastic modulus of the GRP skins
  T is the total thickness of the beam
  c is the core thickness
  d is dimension between skin centrelines
  b is the width of the beam
For thin skins this can be simplified to:–

$$R = \frac{E \times t \times d^2 \times b}{2}$$

where t is the thickness of the skins.
  The actual *deflection* is comprised of two parts, deflection due to bending plus bending due to shear.

Deflection due to bending $= \dfrac{WL^3}{48R}$

Bending due to shear $= \dfrac{W.L.c.}{4.b.d^2.G}$

where W = load
      L = span of beam
      G = modulus of the core
The actual *bending stress* (Sb) in the skins is given by:–

$$S_b = \frac{M.T}{b.t.d^2}$$

where M is the applied bending moment.
The resulting *shear stress* (S$_c$) in the core is then given by:–

$$S_c = \frac{W}{b.d.}$$

Note: These formulas are simplified and neglect any contribution by the flexural rigidity of the core. They will generally give accurate enough results for design purposes, however, especially as a safety factor will be used in designating the design load. If it is required to analyse the flexural rigidity of a sandwich beam including the contribution of the core the complete equation is:–

$$R = \frac{E_s.b.t^3}{6} + \frac{E_s.b.t.d^2}{2} + \frac{E_e.b.c^3}{12}$$

where E_e is the elastic modulus of the core material and t is the thickness of the skins. Again this can be simplified by ignoring the middle term, i.e.

$$R = \frac{E_s.b.t^3}{6} + \frac{E_c.b.c^3}{12}$$

Normally this will give answers with less than 1% error.

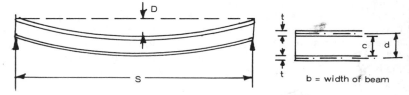

FIG. A8

b = width of beam